Rut to Revival

A Gypsy Soul Nomadic Journey

Linda Mastromonaco

ISBN: 978-0-578-27371-6

Printed in the U.S.A.

Editing: Erin Daniels

Cover Design: Linda Mastromonaco

Acknowledgment

I am most grateful to my children, Derek and Cara, for their unconditional love and concern for my well-being as I embarked on a new beginning. They, along with their spouses and my precious grandchildren, sent me on my way to becoming a nomad with the most generous and thoughtful gifts. I thank God for them, as I would not be who I am if it were not for their love and care.

I'm so thankful for my many friends, and followers of my YouTube channel Serene and Simple Life. Many viewers have provided me with prayers, support, and generous deeds when I needed them most. This nomad journey would not have been the same or as fun if it were not for the friendships birthed along the way. You have offered your land for me to reside on for a while, and opened your hearts in so many ways. God bless you always and in all ways.

This book would not be what it is if it weren't for my rock star editor Erin Daniels who "got me" and was able to help me convey my story clearly and concisely. Erin used her editing talent and gave me the gift of many long hours perfecting this book for publication. Thank you for being there for me and your generous service to those in need.

Most importantly, I thank my Lord and Savior Jesus Christ for His hedge of protection as I traveled this exquisite country, experiencing His handiwork at every turn. I'm humbled that God would provide me with this amazing opportunity to GO SEE DO and to be an encouragement to others searching for their "new beginning" by sharing first-hand knowledge and the fascination of this lifestyle.

Table of Contents

Prologue*

According to an article I read on the internet the average life expectancy is 79.05 years. If I live that long, I have approximately 15.05 years left on Earth. Time is running out yet when you make the most of every day, it's more than enough time to set goals, fulfill dreams, and make a difference. With those statistics, my life is over three quarters behind me, and with one quarter left, God willing, I have my best years yet ahead of me!

My life as a nomad began in September of 2018 when I stepped out into the great unknown to engage the world in a much more direct and hands-on way without the encumbrances and hindrances of a sticks and bricks lifestyle. I had decided to travel the country in my car, sightseeing, working, playing and making my car my new home. On the first leg of my adult journey, I moved several times as a military spouse and realized that staying stationary was not for me. Now, the open highway was again calling out to the gypsy spirit in me.

I feel like I am on the second leg of my journey. The first leg of adulthood involved a marriage of nine years and raising two children, first with a spouse and then providing for them as a single mom, which included having a place we could call home. This period of my life spanned about 29 years. But when my daughter married, my role as a mom ceased to exist as I had known it.

This role of being needed to console, advise or help, as most mothers want to do in their child's life, had faded and I needed to find God's new purpose for me. What is freeing for me now is the realization that all my past experiences have allowed me to come into my own. Although I used to label myself as divorced, I now consider myself as simply single, not only because being divorced feels like a lifetime ago, but also because I know I'm a whole person in Christ, not one who is lacking something because I'm no longer married.

Now that my children have their children, I've moved from a mom role to a grandma of my three sweet peas. Though I love and miss them dearly, I know I have been called to live a life off the grid as a nomad, sharing my experiences, traveling and inspiring others, and helping them to see the possibilities and wonders of God's creation and life. Only God knows how long this season will last, but I know for now it is a calling and not just a lifestyle.

Filling up my gypsy soul is the second leg of my life's journey. And in all honesty, it was a necessary decision for my sanity at the time I chose it for my emotional well-being and finances. My bank account needed to be replenished, and my spirit needed a boost, so my journey began.

This journey has been exciting, to say the least. I've been given another chance to have a new beginning with fresh insights, understanding, and opportunities, and it has opened my eyes to a whole new, authentic way of being and living.

***To access all videos displayed in brackets referenced throughout this book , please go to Serene and Simple Life YouTube channel. You can locate the videos within the channel and in the playlists, organized by topic. This book is also available as an eBook that includes the links.**

With age, comes wisdom.
With travel, comes understanding.

Chapter 1

Before Nomad Life

A New Beginning

The day was no different from any other day except it was Sunday. For many people, whether celebrated on Saturday or Sunday, the Sabbath is to be acknowledged and treated as a time to rest, a day to let go of the hustle-bustle of the week and just chill. "And on the seventh day, God rested," the Bible says. Through the years, this concept has been a difficult one for me. To chill, in my mind, means to do nothing. And I can't just do nothing. I seem to need to do something or be busy no matter what. So, for me, Sundays are no different from any other day. This way of being has warded off loneliness and provided me with a sense of purpose, meaning I need to be productive and accomplish something.

My biggest decision on any given Sunday over the last few years has been whether I want to go to church or skip it. Although once I decide to go to church, I'm happy I made an effort and decision to go. It has been the getting there part I have struggled with because I equated going to church with couples and families. Ever since the empty nest syndrome hit, it has been a challenge to climb out of the slump of going it alone.

This day was the same. I got up, brewed my usual two cups of ordinary coffee, and started moving around in my newest abode, a 17 by 25-foot room I had been renting for approximately six months. For no particular reason, I decided I would go to church. I had wanted to check out a new church nearby anyway. This glorious sun-filled Sunday seemed like a perfect day to do that. Perhaps God had a divine message for me to hear.

I pulled out a cute pair of capris and a colorful top to portray a look of absolute happiness, and off I went to church alone, with my well-trained appearance of being content. Not that anyone cares, so why not put on a front, being miserable takes more effort. If Mr. Right was at church, I was sure he wouldn't be looking for Ms. Down and Out.

When I returned from church to my little one-room abode, I changed into a pair of loose-fitting comfy shorts with a simple tank top and my worn tennis shoes to go on my usual walk down the street and around the park. It was a lovely escape, if only for half an hour. There had been no earth-shattering message at church meant for me today. Despite that, I found the day delightful, although lonely feelings within the four walls usually seemed to be louder and more pronounced on Sundays.

As soon as got back from my walk, I turned on the TV for company. I grabbed a snack and plopped down on my soft gray loveseat with an inward sigh, prepared to while away the hours until 7 p.m. I could justify calling it a day at that magical hour, having endured another 10 hours alone. Routinely, I would snuggle up in bed to watch even more TV until my eyes grew heavy, unbelievably bored with the monotony of it all.

Not wanting to think about my business and its desperate need for a boost in social media marketing, I scrolled through the channels on the remote to find a show I'd be content watching which rarely happened. My mind wandered. Bored to near tears, I stared out the huge window. The cozy little nest I had creatively designed and decorated into sections—kitchen, dining, living, bedroom all in one tiny space cried out to me, "I'm here, but I'm empty."

The window to the outside overlooked my landlady's old, outdated patio furniture, which surrounded her dilapidated pool, now chipping with old paint. The landscaping around it was manicured, though even this did not help shake my inner growing discontent. An occasional hummingbird interrupted the monotony and melancholy of this scene that seemed snatched right out of the 1950s.

The ho-hum doldrums of today and every other day of the week were beginning to wear on me. Was this how the rest of my life was going to play out? Get up, kickstart the day with coffee, putz around my room, eat, chase business, snack, TV, eat again, sleep, repeat? The mere thought of this usual routine frightened me.

Along with trying to make a go of yet another business, would I have to succumb to endless hours on my feet working a side retail job so I could afford to rent a one-room roof over my head? If my health faltered, would there be a chance I would end up destitute while running on the treadmill of life? I shuddered as I realized it was quite possible.

The longer I sat on my little loveseat, the gloomier things became. Suddenly, a wave of initially unrelated yet strangely more connecting thoughts came over me out of the blue. Accompanying those thoughts were feelings of warmth and contentment. It was puzzling, considering I was supposed to be lingering on my depressing thoughts of what the next chapter of my life would look like—a life that had lately begun to run out of meaning and significance. Very strange indeed, as I had not experienced warm, fuzzy feelings for as long as I could remember.

Was this a moment of divine intervention? Was the voice of God I had hoped to hear when I went to church earlier that day now whispering in my ear? The feelings became stronger and stronger, almost to the point of being overwhelming. My heart and mind were suddenly racing with new thoughts and exciting new possibilities.

I knew in my gut that now was the time for a change. It wasn't the furniture rearranging for the 10th time in eight months type of change, but rather one of those huge, monumental, life-changing sorts of epiphanies. You know, one of those changes like marriage, divorce, having a baby, landing a new career, launching a business type of change. Yes, as the cliche goes, I had already been there, done that, on all counts. There I was, alone and depressed. My purpose on earth seemed to be draining from my very soul that had been crying out for change. And God heard my soul's cry, and I said "yes."

A new thing is coming ~ God

Off the Treadmill

These feelings of inspiration were now turning into questions in my mind. The racing thoughts began to blend and become more concrete and certain. God was now speaking, and I was listening. I wondered what the possibility of leaving a lifetime of side gigs to have a roof over my head would look like. Would it be possible to escape the weary treadmill of life? I wasn't sure, but I needed to explore those thoughts more.

A core belief of mine has always been if you want to change your life, you must not sit and talk about it but go ahead and take action. Don't take too much time for contemplation but move with a sense of urgency and intention. Otherwise, you tend to lose interest, talk yourself out of the possibility of real change, or even let someone else do it for you. I have always chosen a doer life over one of being a couch potato, though over time, I had become just that instead of walking my talk.

I have always believed God is in the details of our lives. He plants the thoughts, provides us with the necessary resources, and finally guides us with the action steps if we are open and will take the time to listen to what He is saying.

The resources before me right now were genuinely plentiful. Social media groups, YouTube channels, blogs, and even Pinterest were available to help me set the wheels in motion. I dove into all of it! I typed "living in a van, living in a car" in the search bar of the various social media sites. I was preoccupied finding and sorting through all the available information for days. I found topics on solo women, RV living, van dwellers, car dwellers, and so much more.

My head began to spin with all the new search terms and concepts, and my mind began to awaken from its former doldrums with new vigor and enthusiasm for living. Like a light switch, God took me from dark to light and despair to delight. They say when the student is ready, the teacher will appear. Yes, my Lord and Savior Jesus Christ, my teacher spoke, and I was the hungry student ready to receive.

You could say it was pretty much on the spot, on my tiny loveseat that humid, hot summer day in Texas, when I said YES to living a life on the road as a gypsy nomad. I was elated and excited to realize I was going to travel and see the country in a new and affordable way. No rent or mortgage payments would hinder or dictate my life, and no more confining one-room apartments to tie down my restless spirit.

I've always been open to change because it can lead to growth if you're willing. I realized this would be the epitome of living outside my comfort zone, a thought that might disturb and even stop many from pursuing it. I remember experiencing the feeling of the "peace that passes all understanding" washing over my heart and mind as I pondered the new possibilities on what would become for me a truly life-changing, game-changer sort of day.

Life is short and the world is wide.

Up Until This Day

Before this life-changing day, I had considered going back to school to become a licensed drug and alcohol counselor. Previously, I had applied twice several years apart. The first time was in California, but God placed in my heart that it was not the right time, so I returned all the books to the school and moved to Delaware to get some much-needed emotional healing. The second time was when I returned to California. I applied to a community college but decided against attending due to the high cost.

Although I had stumbled upon some appealing leads to start working in the field of counseling, one by one, the doors kept closing on me. It became clear to me this was not God's will. I felt the Holy Spirit calling me back to Texas where I had lived during the first part of my marriage as a new bride and where I later became a new mom. I thought I would have a second chance at getting my life back on track after relationship heartaches and an unsuccessful career in real estate in California.

Once I moved back to Texas, I considered trying my hand at selling real estate once again. It was a challenging line of work, but I always delighted in a favorable challenge. During the recession of 2008, I had worked hard for two companies, so it made sense to me that I could jump into the new home market without the toil of studying and retaking the test to obtain my real estate license. Not a chance. Everyone I spoke to wanted someone who had direct experience in new home sales. I never understood this then, and I don't understand it now. How do you get the skills needed if no one wants to give you a chance to get the experience? A catch-22 at its finest.

But God wasn't going to leave me hanging. A friend from church told me about a purchasing agent position that had opened at a healthcare company where she worked. I applied and was immediately hired. It was only slightly more money than the minimum wage jobs I held over the years, and thought perhaps this would be my ticket to get ahead financially. But this did not turn out to be the case, as it was mentally taxing with an equally difficult boss. The type of work was also beyond the scope of my knowledge at the time. On top of all that, sitting for eight hours straight was torture for me. Not my cup of tea at all as I'm unable to sit for five minutes, let alone 480 minutes.

Never in my life had I quit anything without giving it a fair shake. Usually, I quit a job only because I was moving. However, I concluded my sanity was worth more than the pain and possible health repercussions of sticking it out. Formerly a no quitter under any circumstances, I now hastily submitted my resignation before my 90-day review was up.

Suddenly, the light bulb came on again. God was talking through this experience. As I began to reflect on my past choices and examined where doors had closed and where relationships and various vocations had not panned out, I began to see God had a bigger plan and a better purpose for my life than I had previously imagined. I had been searching and looking in all the wrong places for years. It was as if I wanted to do things the more traditional and predictable accepted way for most of my life. Just a slow learner, you may be thinking, although I indeed had earned a degree—one in the school of hard knocks.

A gigantic window had flung open for me, and this gypsy nomad now realized she had to step or drive through it. Only this time, it would be God's way instead of what I assumed I needed or should do for all these years.

New month. New beginnings. New opportunities.
New blessings. God is good.

The Back Story

This passion to get up and go didn't evolve overnight. For as long as I can remember, I have had gypsy blood running through my veins. Dad used to lovingly call me a gypsy as I ran around barefoot during all seasons of the year. Perhaps I was born for this very season of my life.

The idea of moving to new locations had always appealed to me. This might have been what attracted me to my former husband at the beginning of our relationship. He was in the military for nine years and moved three times, which appealed to my gypsy soul.

I grew up in a small town in the USA. Irwin, Pennsylvania is 30 miles away from Pittsburgh. One would never think such a settled, predictable upbringing would produce a gypsy nomad mindset. I was the stereotypical middle child.

Mom was a stay-at-home/working mom until we were teenagers, and dad was a hard-working man his entire life. We were your typical, middle-class family. Like most families at the time, we stayed put in the same house in the same neighborhood during my entire childhood and teenage years.

But I was not your typical small-town kid, as I felt like a bit of a black sheep. I was somewhat of a rebel and remember smugly telling my parents when I was 16, that I was planning to move to California as soon as possible and never return. Dad retorted, "you don't want to move to California. California is going to fall in the ocean."

He should have said instead, "let me help you pack your bags." I always wanted to go left if others were going right. And once I started down that path, it never stopped. Some things never change. Yet this can be a positive thing. God uses it all to bring us to a new place.

Some 30 years after this initial announcement, my prediction came true. I made it to California. But you know, they say be careful what you wish for. That move was certainly not without heartaches and financial duress. As it turned out, I spent approximately $190,000 during the following 14 years on rent and mortgage payments, spending six years in California and the remaining eight elsewhere. This was covered mainly by the physically and mentally taxing side jobs I felt compelled to acquire each time I moved.

I now found my gypsy blood running hot, moving 12 times, once every 14 months. This frequent moving around, of course, was no surprise to my friends. Each time I posted on social media about a new state I was moving to, the overall reaction and consensus were, "there she goes again."

But little did I know at the time that the life God was now introducing me to had been beckoning me for years. I just hadn't seen it. Of course, I was not quite ready. I had to undergo more challenges, and painful growth awaited me to adequately prepare me for what was to come. That's how God seems to work.

For me to graduate from this course of the school of hard knocks, I would need to go through some painful experiences before I would be ready to let go of the only type of life I had ever known. After all, it would be a great leap of faith into the unknown to let go of the known comfort and security of four walls. This concept of letting go would not be emotionally driven or merely figuratively speaking. It would need to be literal.

"Normalcy" is a paved road.
It's comfortable to walk.
But no flowers grow there.

Coming Full Circle, Twice!

After moving the second time to California, I finally decided that as beautiful as the state itself was, it was time to move out of California and not look back. It only took me two years to realize I could no longer afford to live there. Besides, who would want to keep paying for sunshine and feeling the pain at the pump regularly!

Yes, Texas was once again beckoning me where I had lived as a new bride. It is known to be a friendly state for business with no state tax, so it seemed a no-brainer to move back. It made complete sense. Only this time, things were different. The debt I had almost obliterated several years earlier was mounting again due to the start of a new, potentially hot business I had recently launched in Arizona after moving there from Delaware.

Though my business began at the Lord's prompting, and it was advantageous to move to California from Arizona to grow it, or at least I speculated it would be, the pace I was choosing to expand it, along with the mounting debt accompanying it, would soon cause me problems.

Of course, it didn't help that apartment rentals averaged $1,600 a month in Arizona, and to stay alive, pay the rent, and keep going, I once again had to succumb to a minimum wage pursuit. Throughout these moves, I worked at Chico's clothing store, Ralph's grocery store, and Cracker Barrel restaurant, to name a few. The same rut as always, or so it seemed. Even doing all that, I was barely keeping up with paying all my bills on time, not to mention the growing debt of my now ever-expanding product line, which would eventually ruin any possible financial security.

I had come to realize I had to finally let go of the possibility of owning another home on my own, as I had three times before. I had been the proud homeowner of property in Pennsylvania, a fairly new three-bedroom manufactured home in Delaware, and an old one-bedroom mobile home in Arizona. Owning a house was now too much of a financial risk, with mounting credit card debt, needing a chunk for a down payment, and having nothing in savings. Even the thought of living in a cozy one-bedroom apartment in a complex with amenities was starting to feel like it was no longer an option.

I had rented small, maid-type quarters attached to a 1950s residence for a mere $875 a month during my second stay in California. I then moved to San Clemente, a charming city by the ocean, to rent a 12 by 12 room in a million-dollar mansion for $850 a month before moving back to Texas. What was I thinking? It now seemed evident that I wasn't. Though this home came with a three-car garage, there were no driveway or garage privileges for me. It became apparent that my only future option might be renting a room for the remaining years of my life. Talk about feeling confined and disheartened. My gypsy nomad soul was in a bit of despair.

The room I now rented in Texas was enormous compared to the room I had left in San Clemente. It was also $250 less per month. A score? Perhaps. Maybe I could get ahead this time, except for the credit card debt, which seemed to keep dogging my efforts to do that. At first, things seemed to be working out well. In the short term, I felt happy and content. I would walk to the park, eat, feed my news and weather junkie addiction, manage my business, go to bed, and repeat. But the financial benefits could not outweigh or overcome the gloom beginning to settle over me.

This was my landlady's house, not mine, to change the ambiance. The decorating style throughout this widow's home was dreary, depressing, and outdated. Tattered encyclopedias and old dusty books from the 1950s lined the shelves. And never was there a curtain drawn or a window opened, as she had bars placed on them for safety. Nor was there any natural way to get fresh air inside. It felt like walking through a dungeon when I passed by her living and family room on the way to my little nest retreat.

The kitchen area, at least, had a cozy appeal though the way I cleaned her stove or didn't, according to her standards, was beginning to take its toll on me. The garage packed full of tools from her late husband of a decade ago prevented me from using it, so my car sat in the driveway. Although I liked my huge, neatly decorated room, the overall atmosphere was depressing. And more importantly, the amount of money I spent on the rent was frustrating and unsettling.

I finally figured out why I was not cut out to live in someone else's place no matter how much money it might save. The walls were closing in on me. I needed to do something different. Otherwise, I knew I would lose my sanity or, as they say, go bonkers.

I decided it was time to start planning and downsizing for this new beginning to become a reality. Off the treadmill into the great unknown, I would venture. My mind raced with ideas. My heart and head were all in and I could hardly wait to make it happen. I would cut out the most significant barrier to getting ahead, my living quarters expense, purchase a minivan to live in, travel the country, expand my business and take up occasional jobs as I wished for new experiences and memories. I set myself a time frame of two and a half months to get everything done I needed to do to step out into a new way of living.

It was July 1, 2018, the day God spoke to me. Not in an audible voice but in a convicting presence that struck my heart and soul about where I needed to go next and what I had to do to fulfill His purpose for my life. It was like a breath of fresh air, reviving my soul and giving me a new zest for life. Then, exactly two and a half months later, as planned, on September 15, 2018, life as I had known it living in a stationary living space would cease to exist. I would continue to have a roof over my head, though now it would be on wheels.

If we were meant to stay in one place,
we'd have roots rather than feet!

Breaking the Bank

Up to this point, I had worked since I was 16 and lived a so-called normal life, or what society deems normal. I also followed society's prescribed steps to success. I graduated high school, received an Associate Degree in business, and married at 23. We bought a home, and by 30, I had two children. It seemed I was doing it all right. The only thing missing was the white picket fence. However, that is where the similarities of normal ended. Another statistic is I was a divorcée at 32 with two small children.

Praise God my parents were only a 20-minute drive away from my new-to-me single-wide, 72-foot-long trailer in a mobile home park. Raising two very young kids on my own would be no easy task being in the direct sales industry. Debt, debt, and more debt encircled me as I strove to build a thriving business. It was a continuation on the treadmill of debt. Little did I know that I would remain there for a long time.

I was a stay-at-home working mother like my mom. The only difference is that I was a single parent for most of my children's upbringing. I managed to do very well with my direct sales business with God providing extraordinary blessings throughout my career. It spanned 23 years, and I ended up in the top four percent of the company of consultants with a fancy "Senior Director" title. Moreover, my Creative Memories® business rewarded me in more ways than one. I earned all-expense-paid trips to exotic places.

Mom and I went to exquisite Santa Barbara and Hollywood, California, for a week on one trip. On another, my daughter and I reveled in a trip to the Virgin Islands. The income was substantial in the later years, and it allowed me to stay at home with my children. That was the icing on the cake.

In the early years of my growing business, the old saying of "robbing Peter to pay Paul" rang true. It's how I stayed afloat as I desperately wanted to provide my children with what I had growing up—a real home. I got caught in a vicious cycle of moving money from high-interest credit cards to zero-interest cards. Yet it kept me from drowning financially and becoming homeless with two kids.

Due to my on-time minimum payments and constant credit card switching to lower interest rate promotions, my credit remained excellent. But that didn't help matters much. As I ran faster and faster on my business-building and credit treadmill, I began to build up inventory and debt at a pace that exceeded the revenue I was taking in.

Of course, the credit card companies reward those of us who do what I did and taunt you with their limitless offers to take the bait. Even worse, my big-picture, visionary-type thinking got in the way and soon failed to line up with the reality of my income and financial statements. This is deceptively easy to do, but now it had happened to me.

The old cliche you must spend money to make money was my belief at that time. I can tell you that it came back to bite me hard. Not wanting to shortchange my children or me, I purchased a real home to fulfill the American dream and enhance my growing business with the idea of being more profitable by having a more efficient and larger workspace to conduct workshops and holiday open houses. I also purchased a reliable, high-end brand-new car with a hefty monthly payment.

There was no shortage of Christmas gifts for the kids. It was exciting to enjoy the fruits of the good fortune I was experiencing and provide some extras for my kids. Spending money that I didn't have on furniture and clothing added to my growing insurmountable debt. An absolute downfall for me is my love for new and nice things. It was easy to get caught up with it all with an ever-growing business. Hindsight being 20/20, I would have done just as well and much better by shopping at thrift stores and not splurging on a new car.

Like many people, I worked extra hard yet never saw myself getting ahead. Why was that? It felt like we were always struggling financially. As my debt mounted, I continued to build my Creative Memories® business to get a handle on my debt to obliterate it. As always, the more money I made in my career, the more easily substantial amounts of new credit were offered to me. Bait and hook.

I think I had over $100,000 in credit available at one point. I always paid the minimum payment on time but hardly ever had any extra to come anywhere near eliminating it. Of course, the new higher credit card interest was killing me after the zero-interest period was up. I was on a fast treadmill to financial ruin—hook, line, and sinker.

And believe me, this situation certainly had not evolved due to a lack of trying, hard work, or having a strong work ethic, or even reasonably good money management. It honestly creeps up on you in the dark, imperceptibly, without you being aware.

After 23 years as an independent consultant in direct sales, I gave birth to another business following my real estate career in California. My Say It Display It® business began in 2015. Once again, I sank tons of money into the business with product, marketing, design, trademarks, and more, hoping to finally create the momentum needed to gain substantial profit in the business, which would set my feet on more secure financial ground.

Work, work, work, and more debt. Profitability did come, but not without the big "B" that came knocking at my door first. And the "B" did not merely stand for "bump," it was the big one. It stood for "bankruptcy."

Never in a million years would I have thought this would be at my doorstep. I could balance a checkbook, run a business, hold a side job, and pay my bills on time each month. I was even able to keep my credit score in the 800s. Unfortunately, I couldn't get off the treadmill I was on and avoid the financial ruin before me. It percolated like an ever-hotter pot of coffee, with one purchase, one business idea, or expense at a time, along with ever-growing inventory stockpiles mounting up, not yet sold. A few too many of these actions I chose were probably not a part of God's "bigger plan" for my life! I could now feel the walls beginning to cave in. The debt was becoming unsustainable.

Constant prayer, phone calls, visiting different law firms, and reading about the subject of bankruptcy on the internet, including what the Bible has to say about it, were my new action steps. I asked God for His all-powerful wisdom about what to do. I succumbed and filed for bankruptcy. Then I asked Him to forgive me. This decision did not come without shame, guilt, restless sleep, and tears.

Six months after making the decision and filing bankruptcy, it was discharged. Over and done with, but not forgotten, my formerly excellent credit score, which I had proudly kept intact for 40 years, was now in shambles. Tears came to my eyes as I wrote this chapter. That is the degree to which this has affected me.

When I was going through this, I thought of my father. I have wondered whether he would be disappointed in me with what I had done and how I got to this point, one purchase, one credit card at a time. He had always preached to us if you can't pay cash for something, you can't afford it. Of course, I had believed that wouldn't necessarily apply to the startup of a business I expected would yield the fruits of its investment. But as you've seen, reality told another story. However, knowing I had made common, honest mistakes eased the pain of my choices and helped me forgive myself for those mistakes.

Of course, the truth is there is never a reward without risk. But I was unaware that it is easy to stretch yourself too thin while building a business and spend beyond your means. It is a slow, deceptive, silent creep that suddenly emerges by surprise. I do not have that answer to why I thought it could not happen to me. It does happen to so many. But if you learn from painful lessons like this one, it can be a blessing in disguise. Perhaps this was God's plan for my life. If I didn't learn my lesson now, when would I?

Some of the bad feelings I was experiencing started to fade as my lawyer explained why we had bankruptcy laws in the first place. He did not want me to feel ashamed or humiliated, as I certainly felt. His wisdom and experience helped me not to be so hard on myself during this time.

However, admittedly the process of filing bankruptcy left a mark of failure on me, which has only gradually faded over time. It helps to know that I'm not alone in this life situation. My writing about the incident here is the first time I have shared this part of my life with the world to know. I was too embarrassed to share this heartache even with my kids. Would they understand at their young age with limited life experiences how this could happen or deem me irresponsible and careless that I let it happen?

I've included this painful part of my journey in case someone out there relates to it and will help them or perhaps can learn from my mistakes. If this is the case, it is well worth retelling the story of how this chapter of my life went from rut to revival.

As a side note, financial experts and even bankruptcy lawyers have said to rebuild your credit, you need to apply for and use new credit. Of course, those are high-interest cards, which I was never accustomed to, with the excellent credit score I had carried. The process requires paying off your debt each month to retain your decent score, which I was also never accustomed to. I'm not convinced such a process does much except get you back on the debt treadmill, something I swore I would never allow happen to me again, and I'm not going to take a chance.

Instead, I now choose to pay cash or do without. My dad tried to teach me that lesson, but obviously, the student wasn't ready to listen and apply his wise advice. It's true, this student seemed to enjoy learning things the hard way, or at least it appeared that way.

Now with bankruptcy behind me, other than the feeling of being confined inside four walls, wanting desperately to get out and let the gypsy soul in me finally have her day, why would I choose to forgo the financial stability of sticks and bricks lifestyle? What about the idea of a house as an investment? What about the usual argument financial advisors give you of emphasizing good debt over bad debt?

Since my business of Say It Display It® has continued to grow and prosper, I figured the best way to quickly realize business profitability would be to eliminate the biggest ball and chain expense most people have—rent or mortgage payments.

However, I'd like to stress the real motivation to pursue a nomad life traveling the country was not financial but personal. Also, I do not claim to be a victim of my circumstances and take responsibility for the collapse of my financial well-being. I made poor choices, wanting to grow my business before it was ripe, spent money in excess, and rationalized my purchases of a new car, furniture, etc., or a bigger pad over a trailer, over being satisfied with what I had been given. A poverty mentality does not plague me either, that I need to live in my car. Plain and simple, I choose to. It is what I have been called to do. You cannot put a price on experiences, be they good or bad.

It is very important to me to lead by example and help others like yourself discover how you could gain a new level of happiness in your life by venturing out in a new and affordable way. I'm not here to "just talk the talk" but to "walk the talk." I'm grateful for the chance to make a difference in another person's life.

In videos on my YouTube channel, I've often mentioned this lifestyle is truly about living life large. This completely new way of managing my life was what I was called to do and the perfect expression of my gypsy nomad nature. With God, there is no coincidence, but a God-incidence.

The financial and personal events, however difficult they may have seemed, created the perfect happy accident of bringing me to the place where God would open my eyes to the most exciting possibilities I could ever imagine.

I want to share words I read once, "Sometimes we must hurt to grow. Sometimes we must fail to know. Sometimes we must lose to gain. Because some life lessons are best learned the hard way."

This lesson of going through bankruptcy was growth for me. This season brought me to the blissful path my life is now on.

Earth has no sorrow that heaven cannot heal.

Chapter 2

Preparation for New Lifestyle

Setting the Plan in Motion ~ Research and Lists

My mind was racing with the to-do list of tasks I'd have to complete over the next two and a half months. I set a deadline for myself to pursue this new way of life. I wanted to live off the grid as much as possible so I could GO SEE DO.

I needed to consider not only what to do, but also how to do it. Life without modern refrigeration, quick and easy microwave meals I had become accustomed to, a handy toilet (especially for emergencies), easily accessible showers, and even life without the background noise of a TV seemed like daunting obstacles I would need to overcome.

Of course, I was always up for a challenge, not the kind where you jump out of a plane, but the kind where you must think outside the box. These types of challenges always make me want to take a chance and try something new. I'd have to take each of these modern conveniences one by one and find a different way to manage my life.

It didn't take long for me to realize YouTube would be my online library for finding answers to all the "how what, and where" questions I'd be facing. What do you eat if you don't have access to refrigeration? Where do you take your showers? How do you run your business? Even something as simple as what to do on a bad weather day without a TV to keep you entertained was a question I had.

The first tangible thing I did was to purchase a notebook in which I could organize and record everything I learned about this nomadic lifestyle. As I gathered information, I jotted down tips, hints, and tricks on the various subject pages—food, hygiene, and sleeping arrangements. The more information I gathered, the more I realized there was to learn. It was energizing and I felt alive. It was the first time in a long time I had felt these emotions.

Creating a wish list of my wants and needs was something I did daily. Shopping for things on the internet took up a lot of time. Who knew there were so many options for basic items like a dressing room tent, a travel pillow, and emergency supplies! Even an all-in-one earth-friendly shampoo/cleanser combination made the list. However, I wasn't buying anything yet, I was only window shopping. When the time came to make a purchase, I would pay with cash or nothing at all.

Researching power options was the most difficult task I faced. When it came to understanding lead or lithium batteries, inverters, converters, AC or DC, and 12 volts, my brain hurt. It all jumbled up in my head like a tangle of fried wires.

Being a lifelong information gatherer, I asked a million questions of my cyber friends in the countless groups I joined on social media sites. What do I need to power a laptop, iPad, phone, and possibly a fridge? How much wattage would be needed for each? For solar, how do you convert amps to watts, or do you even do that? The number of possible answers and options was equal to the number of questions I had. I'm not certain I'd be able to convey specific details to someone else about what they would need for their devices, but I did learn what I needed and am now able to share with others on my channel.

The next item on my to-do list was to narrow down the type of rig I'd like to live in. It was a little stressful for me to consider navigating anything larger than a minivan, so I made a quick decision. I'd build out a minivan, complete with a bed platform. After doing some more research and weighing the various options, I decided on a Toyota Sienna would be the best choice or so I thought. Not so fast.

It would be another six weeks before I began seriously looking for my future home on wheels. In the meantime, I started thinking about what my bed design would look like. It seemed logical to me to simply purchase a cot and use foam as a mattress. A "no-build build," as they call it. I was being true to my keep it simple motto that would serve as my guide for everything in my new life, starting with the title of my YouTube channel, Serene and Simple Life©. Within 14 weeks I was able to make a concise plan and execute it methodically.

To live is the rarest thing in the world.
Most people just exist.

Action Steps ~ Organizing and Selling

It was now time to put the list-making and research mode aside and start taking action. As I looked around the cozy quarters I had created, complete with kitchen, dining, living, and sleeping stations, I wondered how I would possibly be able to rid myself of all the stuff without cramming it all into a storage unit where it would do nothing except cost me money.

It turned out the task was not as bad as I had anticipated. I reminded myself I had downsized no less than 15 times in my life, each time to a different dwelling or apartment, so dismantling a 17 by 25-foot room would be a breeze in comparison. It also wouldn't be that expensive to store a few items. I now realized that all along, God had been preparing the way for me.

Moving on to the next to-do, I wrote down the furniture I'd sell and tagged each piece with a price. It was simple to list the no-brainer items to sell, such as a microwave, a dorm-size fridge, an adorable newly painted kitchen table with four chairs purchased at a consignment shop, a like-new, slim kitchen cart, modern-looking white bookshelves, and a contemporary loveseat. Selling my bed frame with a pricey mattress was still in the "unknown" category.

A couple of apps, Craigslist and Facebook were my go-to's to start to eliminate stuff and make a few quick bucks. I estimated I would make about half the money needed to buy the vehicle I would need so I could go live life large. My credit score was in shambles, so cash was king. Since I'd turned the page on my life and was embarking on a no-debt journey, I was truly inspired to live a debt-free life for the rest of my life.

Oh, for the love of clothes, shoes, books, kitchenware, and knick-knacks. Now the real work was about to begin. Fortunately, I have a ball organizing, sorting, making piles, and playing store. I was now off to work. My obsession with organizing stuff in containers, developed over the course of 30+ years of moving to new places, was going to come in handy.

To begin the process of detaching from stuff I pulled everything out of my drawers, two closets, and underneath my bed. I labeled bins for "toss," "giveaway," and "sell." Over the final months before the scheduled drive off into the great unknown, I visited and revisited the myriad of items daily. I'd look at something and then figure out which category it belonged in. I also allowed myself to change my mind, which usually resulted in a better outcome.

I discovered the longer I stared at the substantial collection of items, the less value and meaning they had for me. When I realized how little I used an item, how much it evoked bittersweet memories of days gone by, or whether it had lost its meaning and significance in my life, I was more easily able to detach and let it go.

In this round of elimination, I gave away at least five bags and boxes of what had once been treasures to me. As mentioned earlier, I had a lot of practice with this purge and toss process over the years.

The large kitchen pieces were sold early in the selling process. This was not an issue for me because I had been able to go into my landlady's kitchen and use her fridge and microwave. Larger pieces such as the loveseat I planned to keep for a while were put up for sale later. I wasn't ready to spend the last two months of my life in my room sitting on an heirloom rocker that I would not be selling.

Three weeks before this scheduled move-out day, I had conducted garage sales on two consecutive Fridays and Saturdays. 80% of my belongings were sold or given away. Amazingly, the morning I left for my new beginning, I had sold every piece of furniture I had wanted to sell, including my bed on the day I moved out of my room. How's that for God's perfect timing! Perfect indeed.

Guess what? I made over $3,000 from those two sales. Not too shabby, considering I thought I had downsized to the bare bones with my move from California to Texas. Little did I know the money from the sale would be my initial buffer savings, which was the first time in a very long time I had money in the bank.

Next, I rented a nearby 7 by10 storage unit. The inventory I sell in my business and the display props/tables I use to set up my store at artist and craft shows took up 80% of that space. The rest of the stuff consisted of a minimal amount of clothes, holiday/miscellaneous decorations, scrapbooks, and random memorabilia I separated into their bins.

Besides the Texas rocker that's wrapped with precious memories of where I nursed and rocked my babies to sleep, I held onto a wrought iron coat rack given to me as a housewarming gift from my son and daughter-in-law. I kept a contemporary metal shelf that folds flat, plus a couple of valuable oak accent tables handcrafted by the Amish in Pennsylvania, where I raised my kids.

I would save these special items for when the time came for me to pay cash for a landing zone—a tiny country cabin where I can regroup, rest and re-energize away from the open road. Although I'll never stop being a GO SEE DO girl, I do want to occasionally rest my feet and sit a spell, as they say in the south, now and then.

He is the richest who is content with the least, for content is the wealth of nature ~ Socrates

---

Rig Choice ~ Life on the Road

Everything seemed to be falling into place. However, how would I be able to get a decent minivan and pay cash for it? I think I had $9,000 in my bank account at the time, with a large portion of that coming from selling almost everything I owned. If I spent all my earnings on a new "home on wheels," I'd be broke with no savings once again. I was all too familiar with that life and didn't want to go back there.

I investigated financing for a brief moment. Thank goodness I was able to snap out of that in a hurry and it was only for a minute! I had looked on Craigslist, Auto Trader, CarMax, and everywhere else I could think of to find my new rig. It was now getting down to the last couple of weeks before my move-out and departure date. Of course, I'd given my landlady the customary 30-day notice as there was no way I would ever forfeit a security deposit.

Then, two decent-looking minivans appeared online. One of the minivans was advertised by an individual owner on Craigslist, while the other was at a dealership. I would try to snatch a deal and have a tiny bit of money left over. But twice I went out ready to make a serious offer, and both times the deal fell through. Both of my vehicles were sold out from under me.

"What do you want me to do, Lord," I suddenly found myself crying out in frustration. He whispered very clearly to me, "I want you to be content with what you have." Was He referring to the Acura I bought brand new in 2003, a car that had now been driven for 16 years? The car had put me in serious debt by requiring a monthly payment of $500 for four years that had been paid in full 12 years ago. That car? It couldn't possibly be what He meant.

Oh, but that was exactly what He meant. My home on wheels would be the well-kept, dependable vehicle that had served me well for all those years of financial struggle. A car that was completely paid off and all mine.

After the initial dismay and shock, I came to terms with the realization I would be living full-time in my 2003 Acura TL (Touring Luxury) sedan. It was no longer as luxurious as it once was, but it still ran like new. I swiftly shifted gears and started planning the bed and layout for it, and gave her the name "Serenity Sedan." I was suddenly in a perfect state of bliss, and I was more excited than ever. Remember how I shared that I dig a good challenge? God has never said anything He didn't mean. He was aware of what He was doing and more importantly what I needed. {Methodical decision to live in my car}

In retrospect, God had been carefully guarding my finances and the management of my money since that fateful "B" day. He wasn't going to allow me to wipe out the little money I had and hit the road virtually broke. All I can say now is praise God from whom all blessings flow! Let His will be done, not mine.

It was now time to say goodbye to an accustomed lifestyle inside four walls and embrace a new beginning. The old faithful and trusty Acura would be my new familiar home and I was ready.

I turned my "can nots" into "cans," and my dreams into plans.

A New Day! – Making It All Work

The big day for a new beginning had arrived. I woke up at the crack of dawn to get the show on the road. The first item on my to-do list was to release my all too familiar retreat to its new owner. Parting was sweet sorrow, but not really. At this point, I no longer needed a bed or even desired one. Over the past couple of years, I had been struggling with a mystery pain throughout the night when turning from side to side. Doctors had no explanation.

With no real diagnosis, I decided to live with it with the help of a heating pad to relax my aching muscles. Adios to a bed, possibly for the rest of my life, though I've learned to never say never. The buyer of the bed arrived promptly and gave me the full asking price. He was then off to his daughter's college dorm room with his new purchase.

Now, where would I sleep? I had decided weeks earlier that sleeping in the back seat of my car would not be favorable. Not only because of the unevenness of the back seat and the hump in the center but also for the same reason lying in a bed wasn't comfortable for me due to the mysterious pain that took a significant time in the morning to undo. What to do, what to do? To solve this dilemma, I acted out the story of *Goldilocks and the Three Bears* by trying out various "beds" in the car.

After a lot of trial and error, I realized the driver's seat would be the best option for a bed, having experimented with the back seat and the passenger front seat. The steering wheel would serve as a gripper bar for my nightly tossing and turning. My passenger seat would be utilized for housing necessities without a daily shuffle and rearranging for nighttime. Not to mention no longer having to deal with the discomfort that comes with lying in a vertical position. I was relieved to discover the solution was so simple. "Lord, you do understand our every need." I felt revitalized and ready to embark on this new journey the Lord had planned for me.

Next, the interior was meticulously divided into four sections as part of its four-part organizational structure. On the front passenger seat was a food section packed in one of four new soft-side boxes. The huge back seat contained a 3-drawer unit purchased at Joann Fabrics, a craft box, a jacket box, and five mesh clothing bags, all organized according to the type of clothing. The 3-drawer unit contained kitchen necessities in two of the drawers, while the third was a miscellaneous catch-all drawer. Perfection. My life's necessities were now all prioritized in the confines of my car and easily accessible from the front seat!

On the floor in the back, I kept canned food on one side and shoes on the other side (behind the driver's seat). My all-in-one power bank, 12-volt hot water pot, and a small, soft-sided insulated lunch box were located on the floor of the front passenger seat. In the trunk, I stored what I call the "outta sight outta mind" items. These were items such as my Say It Display It® product line that I needed to fill online orders or in person, a folding table, a dressing room tent, seasonal clothing, and a propane/butane one burner stove.

The trunk space is what nomads refer to as the garage. Except for my business product, these garage items would be part of my outdoor home when residing on Bureau of Land Management (BLM) land, which was typically for five to 14 days maximum.

It did take a few weeks to master these well-thought-out details. However, when I went to bed at night and upon waking in the morning, I was now able to reach everything from the driver's seat. It was sheer delight. I had no idea at the time that over the course of the next year, I would have the opportunity to confidently show off this "make sense" simple setup to other nomads. With a simple less is more mindset, I truly wanted to empower, encourage and inspire others.

It was pleasing to me when people would say, "You look like you are traveling, not living in your car." I did not have any shame or embarrassment living this way. It has genuinely felt right living in it and having a neat and well-organized travel look and style. My organizational skills were put to excellent use, allowing me to live a minimalist nomad lifestyle. Sharing with others was a bonus with the hope of inspiring them to do the same if they so desired.

When people reacted with enthusiasm and surprise that it could be done so simply and conveniently, I felt even more motivated to keep going and share what I had learned. It became the emotional fuel for my new nomadic lifestyle. I felt like God was putting me in a position to make a difference. I was regaining my sense of purpose in life. Everything now felt right and good.

{Living in my Acura: my nest}

{Part II: Up close and personal in my nest}

Create your happiness. Today is the day.

Minimalism as a Nomad

Being a minimalist or living a life of minimalism is a unique challenge. Learning about and adopting a minimalist lifestyle had a special meaning for me because you can only fit so much of your life's accumulation of things into a car. If you don't want to spend your days rummaging through things, looking for and even losing stuff daily, it is imperative to scale down your life items to only what is necessary to sustain yourself.

Sustaining yourself includes not only your physical self, but also your mental, emotional, and spiritual selves. To achieve the goal of what's required for your comfort level to feel gratified, what you go with may be vastly different from mine.

Here are a few questions to get you started on what you may or may not need to take with you as a nomad:

- Would you like to carry a few photos of loved ones to satisfy the emotional need of holding a photo instead of looking at them on a phone?
- Do you like reading your Bible from an app or an actual book?
- What mentally stimulates you that you'd like to have with you (a few books, puzzles, games) or can you manage this need from your phone?

When I first started on the quest to become a minimalist, I went to the internet to learn more about the subject. I discovered some interesting and alarming statistics. Did you know the average American home has 300,000 items in it, and the average man owns 12 pairs of shoes while the average woman owns a whopping 27 pairs?

A minimalist, according to the definition and understanding I came across, prefers the minimal amount or degree of something. Another definition described this type of person as someone who prefers to keep things very simple. Being a minimalist implies you place a higher value on yourself than on material possessions. It entails making decisions based on what you require rather than on what you desire.

However, this does not imply the items you purchase are inexpensive. A person can decide how much, or little, of a simple lifestyle they want to lead. They can also do it in stages. It is about living with fewer goods. This includes fewer financial burdens such as debt and unnecessary expenses. For many, the philosophy is about getting rid of unnecessary possessions and living a life based on experiences rather than material goods.

There are three top reasons why I wanted to become a minimalist:

1. It provides the opportunity to have a simple lifestyle.
2. Would have less stress, i.e., less stuff = less stress.
3. A way to enhance my serenity.

My goal was to encounter different surroundings and sights and make new friends, with the bonus of saving lots of money by not having an excess of things. This all allowed me to have fresh encounters, and the freedom to not be attached to things. As a result, I can truly undergo a serene and simple life.

Some key motivators helped to make this lifestyle a reality. Over the previous 20 years, I had held many garage and yard sales. My most recent yard sale—that I hoped would be my last one ever featured some of my nicer items, which I'd been moving around for too many years to count.

Before I tried to sell anything, I first reached out to my daughter to see if she wanted any of my better stuff.

If she said "yes" this would provide a way for me to still have some memories around when I would visit her home. I texted her multiple times with photos of these "nicer items." Each time she texted me back three simple words. "No, thank you." Eventually, I caught on. She did not want anything of mine. Nada. Nothing.

I'll admit, I'm not the quickest of learners. Her response to me stung for a few moments, but then I had to let it go. Perhaps she had already caught on to how to live a minimalist lifestyle while I had a ways to go.

The other motivation to downsize to what I believed to be next to nothing was a phone conversation I had with my brother. We seldom talk, but when we do, we play catch up for a bit. I knew he had been retired for quite a few months from a career spanning 40-plus years. I asked him how his retirement was going. He proceeded to share how he had spent the first six months cleaning out his mother-in-law's place. Wow! Six months. This was depressing news that I was not expecting. I thought he would be telling me he was out doing what he always luxuriated in, things like boating and golfing. It was sad for me to learn how the early days of his retirement were playing out.

Around this time I made a conscious decision to not be a burden to my children or their spouses. When I leave this earth, hopefully, they will be able to scoop up my tiny cabin belongings in a few hours and be done with the task of clearing me out.

The real downsizing journey had begun when I moved out of a 3-bedroom house in Pennsylvania and drove to California with my daughter. We quickly realized we would be unable to fit all our possessions into a 750-square-foot, 2-bedroom apartment with a garage in California, so I sold some of the larger pieces of furniture. But even then, we still had a packed garage in CA with barely enough room for my car.

To maintain this new lifestyle, with each item I now owned, there were several questions I would ask myself. "Is this item something I've used in the last 90 days?" "Will I make use of the item in the next 90 days?" "Does this item give my life meaning?" If my response was "no," it was time to bid farewell to the item. Of course, in the preceding years, I had rarely, if ever, asked myself these critical questions or had simply assumed the item met the criteria when it did not. Being honest with yourself requires effort and a great deal of insight.

Conducting garage and yard sales was a fun way to pass the time. Growing up, my sister and I used to get a kick out of playing "store". Not surprisingly, retail or food service have always been my go-to grinds. Yes, it was a marvelous time holding yard sales. The quick cash was my why motivator. It was awesome meeting the lookers and buyers and ultimately feeling a sense of calm in letting go as my belongings found new homes with those who would benefit from their purchase. Or did they?

Some shared what they intended to do with the item or how they would use it. I remember one customer who purchased many of my handy Longaberger baskets I had accumulated over the years and told me she was going to use them as part of the decor at her daughter's wedding. Hearing that made it a little easier about letting them go. Now, when I remember those baskets, I would be at ease knowing they most likely hold wonderful memories for someone else in their new surroundings.

A disturbing thought crossed my mind. Is it possible I was also fueling their desire for more stuff? It concerned me at first, but then I realized it wasn't my responsibility to deal with their decision. It wasn't my business. So, I wasn't going to play counselor to my customers. Instead, I would be satisfied being a store clerk.

Memorabilia has always been the most difficult of all my various keepers to deal with. After all, I'd made a living teaching others how to save and preserve their photographs and memories for future enjoyment. How could I possibly part with a treasured piece of artwork from my children's school days, or a note or card they had written to me?

Realizing I didn't need to keep every single item that had their fingerprints on it was a breakthrough for me. In my mind, it was helpful to return to the when I die scenario in my mind of either leaving a heap for my children to deal with when I died or tackling the mountain right now. I opted for the latter.

I'll never forget moving from Pennsylvania to California and the movers saying to me, "You have a very heavy life." At the time, I was moving every scrapbook I'd ever made, as well as thousands of copies of my autobiography, which I'd published a couple of years before. I had anticipated selling all of them and making enough money to pay off my debt. Unfortunately, eliminating debt through book sales did not happen. I guess you could say this was another one of my "big picture" hopes and dreams gone awry. Years later, I ended up taking them to the dumpster and relinquishing them to the incinerator or landfill.

Of course, I had saved everything that had any happy memories attached to it such as my children's drawings, cards, letters, concert ticket stubs, you name it. The list went on and on. I had over 60 completed scrapbooks, as well as a few plastic bins of various sizes filled with momentums to revisit.

It took me days and days to go through the albums, tossing loose scrapbook pages and photographing hundreds of pages within the albums I was dismantling. It was sheer agony. My children had no desire for my memories and albums. They had their mountain of scrapbooks I had created for them years earlier and given to them as adults to do with as they pleased. It's funny now, but I've never looked at all the photos I took of those scrapbook pages either.

This process of memorabilia elimination went on over the course of a few moves. I would hit a brick wall and couldn't look at another letter from mom or a heartwarming note from my daughter from years ago. Perhaps it was because mom is in Heaven and my daughter had grown up, moved out, and started her own life at a pace that had happened way too fast for me.

My storage unit was a perfect size. When I returned there to fill Say It Display It® orders after a year, I tackled my belongings again over the course of 50-plus hours. This necessitated a few trips to thrift stores and even filling a few bags for the trash. Fortunately, I'm getting close to the point where everything I own is a keeper. I did a quick go-over the day I closed the unit down for good, then I loaded it into a moving pod to be delivered to where my future landing zone would be.

If you're wondering how I was able to downsize and how being a minimalist can serve you, check out this list I found from The Minimalists on YouTube:

- Eliminate discontent
- Reclaim your time
- Live in the moment
- Pursue your passions
- Discover your missions
- Experience real freedom
- Create more, consume less
- Focus on your health
- Grow as individuals
- Contribute beyond yourselves
- Rid yourself of excess stuff
- Discover purpose in your life

And as a bonus, here are some of my Serene and Simple practical tips:

- Just start. Make four piles: give away, sell, toss, keep.
- Carve out small chunks of time so as not to overwhelm yourself and interrupt your decision-making process.
- Have a sale and buy something you need with the earnings. For example, sell something and make a profit of $300. This would buy you a reliable basic solar kit for your journey. A smart purchase like this will give you extra motivation to let go of even more.
- Write down your "Why?" Why are you wanting to downsize and live as a minimalist?
- Commit to giving away one box or one bag per week. Of course, this goal could be two, three, or more bags depending on how much stuff you must get rid of.

To sum up the goal of minimalism or becoming a minimalist in one sentence: Minimalism is a tool to rid yourself of life's excess in favor of focusing on what is important, so you can find happiness - fulfillment - and freedom.

Fill your life with experiences, not things.
Have stories to tell, not stuff to show.

The "What-if" Syndrome

As I set out into the big, wide world—the unknown, many participants in social media groups targeted for nomads and "wannabes" expressed their concerns and uneasy thoughts. They asked questions such as, "What if you break down? What if you get sick? What if you find yourself in a disturbing situation?" What if, what if, what if?

These questions were worth pondering for a minute. What would I do? It occurred to me the same what-if questions curious seekers ask can be asked of anyone who chooses society's normal choice of living in a house or as the term coined by nomads—"sticks and bricks." We all know society considers it to be the normal way to live. But for some reason, we never focus on or question these particular what-ifs when we're confined to a house.

Let's look at each of these challenges separately, and I'll share my thoughts on what you can do or how you might handle each one as they come up.

"What if you break down?" My answer would depend on where I'm at as to what I should/would do. Depending upon that answer:

- Call AAA and sign up for their services on the spot
- Use my car insurance policy to get a tow
- Are there friends, family, or neighbors nearby?

Moving your belongings from your broken down or wrecked rig to a rental car can be inconvenient. I remind them any car inconvenience is like living in a regular home in that you will do what you need to do at the time it occurs. With this mindset, it's not something I need to be concerned about or figure out until it happens.

For example, after only six weeks of ownership in my new-to-me SUV, I had a minor bumper accident (self-inflicted) which happened to me 15 months out as a nomad. Now what? As it turned out, it needed to be in the shop for four days.

Thankfully, God provided me with an entirely unexpected, new friend, (Judy) who offered me the opportunity to stay in her Airbnb while my car was being repaired. I could never have predicted what I would do in this situation. But God knew.

"What happens if you get very ill?" Judy was asked this question and shared with me her response. "I would do the same thing I would do in sticks and bricks. Call 911," she said to whomever. This pretty much sums up my response. If I wasn't feeling well, I simply stopped my wheels, prayed, and let it pass.

If I needed easy access to a restroom, I would park at a truck stop, or a rest area, to have access day or night. When confronted with unexpected circumstances, you do what you must do at the moment. To me, it's a waste of time and energy to try to predict how things will turn out or how you'll handle any given situation, beforehand.

My faith gives me the peace and joy of knowing God has already solved any problem or challenge I may face. If we call on Him, He will provide wisdom and insight into our troubling situation. Amid adversity, we sometimes receive unexpected gifts, such as my new friend who invited me to stay with her for free in her Airbnb.

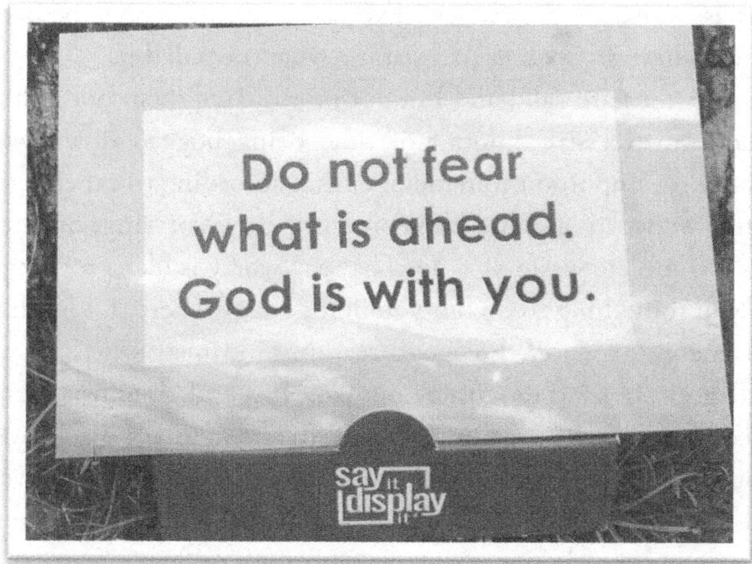

I think the last "what if" to figure out is the easiest one to answer. "What do you do if you find yourself in a disturbing situation?" This inquiry goes hand in hand with the "aren't you afraid" question. In this mobile lifestyle, the answer is very simple, you just turn on the key and drive on.

Here is a valid question for those of you living in sticks and bricks. "What do you do if an uncomfortable-looking or acting person comes knocking on your door? Do you hide under your bed or in your closet? Do you grab your loaded gun?" You cannot leave your house with just the turn of a key when someone is lurking outside or at your door, as I can in my getaway vehicle. So, in a way, nomads have an advantage over those living in sticks and bricks to move away from trouble and not be trapped by someone who may be trying to harm them.

I've often wondered why no one seems to ask us if we are afraid of living in a traditional home—though it seems to be one of the first questions that come up when we deviate from the norm. As you travel, take heart in the fact that statistically, more bad things happen in peoples' homes than anywhere else. Throughout my life, I have experienced firsthand how humankind is fundamentally good. Not only are they good, but you can find them everywhere—neighbors, acquaintances, co-workers, friends, business associates, and strangers. I've had a few lifesaver-type people in my life who have stepped in to assist me when I needed it.

The questions are valid and I'm not minimizing them but I choose to not spend an excessive amount of time being bogged down with the unknowns. It's important to remember that according to experts, most of the things we worry about never come to pass. Worrying, on the other hand, is a complete waste of time. They say worry is like a rocking chair. It gives you something to do but you don't go anywhere. I don't have the time or energy to worry. For good reason, God instructs us to walk in faith. He goes ahead of us with all our concerns and circumstances.

I encourage you to put your trust in Him and deny the devil any power over your life because if you don't, the what-ifs can easily take over your life and prevent you from living it to the fullest. Of course, it's up to you whether or not you choose to activate your faith or live in fear.

Is it possible I'm just a braver person in general? Or, to put it another way, does living in a car require bravery? I don't think it does. *Merriam-Webster* dictionary defines bravery as "the quality or state of having or showing mental or moral strength to face danger, fear, or difficulty." Firefighters, first responders, police officers, the military, and paramedics all fall into the brave category. It's the people who put their life on the line for us, some daily, who are brave. These are the ones facing danger, fear, or difficulty that I give the "bravery" badge. {Bravery Faith Trust}

So, it's not that I'm brave. I simply choose faith over fear. Faith is defined as having complete trust or confidence in someone or something. Trust is defined as a firm belief in the reliability, truth, ability, or strength of someone or something. My Lord and Savior, Jesus goes with me wherever I go.

Faith and trust go hand in hand. When you embrace both, then fear melts away. Refuse to let the feeling of not being brave enough to live as a nomad take hold of you.

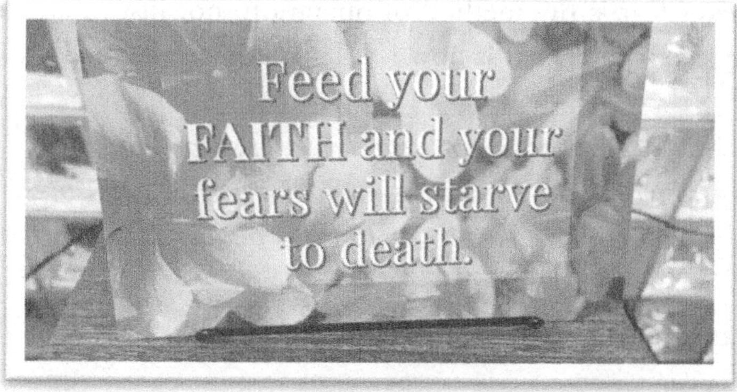

Part of having faith involves common sense and using the resources available to us. For example, I carry practical items for an emergency, such as pepper spray, ropes, a pocket knife, and a hammer. My son gave me a seven-in-one emergency tool, tire gauge, and a shovel for Christmas my first year out. He highly recommended I get a pocketknife so I did. These items, and others I have found useful, are found in my Amazon store. {My Amazon store}

It's true, I completely trust the one who made and cares for me to guide me on my journey, and I have faith He will keep me safe, or at the very least, provide me with the knowledge of what to do in unforeseen circumstances. Whatever your beliefs are, I pray you will not allow fear and worry to rule or control any aspect of your life. Fear will steal your joy and prevent you from living your best life. Period.

Faith over fear is my method of operation, not just in an emergency but all day every day. That is how I roll—on down the road.

Fear does not stop death. It stops life.
And worry does not take away tomorrow's troubles,
it takes away today's peace.

Stealth as Stealth Can Be

Whether in the city, off the interstate, or on BLM land, I like the feeling of being stealthy and somewhat invisible in my rig, even when I'm only hanging out for the day. As mentioned earlier, when another sees my abode or meets me for the first time, they don't know whether I am living in my vehicle or traveling around. Of course, I relish sharing what I'm doing and how I'm living, though not until I get that trusting gut feeling inside me that it's okay to share these details with them.

Good ole' *Merriam Webster* defines stealth as being "furtive, attempting to avoid notice or attention or unobtrusive." Stealth also means "sneakiness." I don't consider myself a sneaky person though I'm not looking to bring attention to myself either. Well, in that case, I guess in these instances I am sneaky.

The concept is slightly different within the realm of what is referred to as stealth camping. Stealth camping is the act of secretly camping in a public or private area and moving on the next morning without being detected.

I learned a few things as I researched and learned more about being stealthy and what to do. If you decide to become a nomad part- or full-time, there are some simple steps you can take to manage stealthiness on your journey.

Keep your rig washed and the interior clean. If a passerby glances inside or you get a knock from security or police, you want to look like you are a stable individual who takes care of your things.

Keep yourself clean. It's all about that first impression. They say people make a judgment about you within 20 seconds. The belief is if you can't or aren't caring for yourself, then others won't trust you to care for their streets or parking lots either.

Arrive late, leave early. This is a rule of thumb, especially if you are parking on a street near apartments, or hotel parking lots. I have arrived in the mid-afternoon at a Walmart, interstate rest area, or a truck stop because I was done driving for the day and wanted to chill. I wouldn't hang out in residential areas all day and give passersby, kids, or neighbors the idea you don't belong and the opportunity to question your presence.

Once you are settled, keep lights and electronics to a minimum. Once again, it depends on where you are. I have gone outside my car to see what the inside looks like when I have my overhead lights on. I couldn't tell there was a light on unless you put your nose right up to the windshield where my commercially made shade cover fits. I also purchased an accordion Reflectix at Walmart to double-duty the windshield and make it darker inside for sleeping. The Reflectix I made for the sides and back window are solid black and fit perfectly to eliminate any peek holes. {Making Reflectix window coverings}

Common sense helps. To be stealthy you do not want to park in close-knit neighborhoods where everyone knows everyone else, or they will know your rig doesn't belong there. Don't park in gated communities or places where all the residents' vehicles seem to be in their driveways or their garages because your vehicle in the street would stand out.

Be respectful. Don't stealth camp in a commercial parking lot like Walmart, Lowe's, or Bass Pro and set up a lawn chair outside. These are not places to camp but places to get a satisfactory night's sleep and move on the next day.

Starting out living in a car and now living in an SUV makes being stealthy so much easier than living in big rigs, cargo vans, RVs, and camper trucks. I don't have stickers, decals, large text, bright colors, a bike, a kayak, a generator, vent fans, or solar panels. I look like 90% of vehicles on the road who are going from point A to point B.

Let me assure you, the more you practice your nighttime routine the easier it becomes. You will move more efficiently and quicker to tuck yourself in, close your curtains by popping your window coverings in place, staying quiet and relatively still within your rig.

Experience joy in the journey.

Window Coverings

I have created window coverings on two separate occasions for each vehicle I lived in since I began my full-time journey into the great unknown. At this point, I think I'm as stealthy as stealth can be. Before I made the first set of five window coverings, I watched quite a few how-to videos on YouTube. I also asked a lot of questions about other people's experiences on Facebook groups.

It's not a hard task. The trickiest part is doing the measuring. The second go-round was quite a bit less stressful. Here's a list of the supplies I used:

- A roll of Reflectix (I purchased a large roll at Lowe's. There was enough left over from the first set to make my second set)
- E6000 glue (first set) or spray can of glue (second set)
- Black felt (first set) or black fabric with vinyl backing (second set)
- Scissors
- Tape measure
- Sharpie marker

Instructions:

1. Cut rectangular shapes of Reflectix larger than the windows by six or more inches.
2. Place the rectangular shape of the reflective material into your window and trace the window onto the material with a Sharpie marker, a couple of inches beyond the window.
3. Cut inside the marker line so you get rid of the marker line. Push the measured reflective material into the window from inside your rig to see if you need to trim a little bit more.
4. Lay black-out fabric or felt on the floor, place measured Reflectix coverings on top, use spray glue on the insulation, one window covering at a time (less smell than the product E6000, though may not be as long-lasting), and secure to felt or fabric.
5. Let dry according to glue directions. I used cans as weights to adhere the fabric to the Reflectix overnight. The second set I made inside my storage unit hallway. I did not leave them to set overnight in the hall. I stored them once I trimmed them (step six) inside my rig overnight to dry.
6. Cut out your window coverings. I left a half-inch of fabric all the way around in case I miscalculated when I did the final trimming.

Additional step: If you choose, you may create a finished edge look by folding over half an inch of fabric and then using black electrical tape to adhere fabric to the insulation for a finished double bond, like when you use bias tape to create a finished edge.

{Stealth as stealth can be}

Chapter 3

Living the Nomad Life

A New Home Hunt Every Night

One of the preconceived notions people make about this way of life is looking for a place to sleep every night is going to be stressful and hard. Of course, it's an important consideration, but it doesn't have to be that way or allow it to consume you. One of the reasons I sought this lifestyle is so I could savor each moment and embrace each day, so I've learned to accept the fact I won't know exactly where I'll be overnighting until later in the day and look at it as a cool hunt to find the perfect stop for the night. I like surprises too!

To alleviate undue stress, there were times I wrote down a rough agenda including what I wanted to GO SEE DO, and an estimate of how many miles that entailed. I'd go on my hunt for a place to spend the night once I was about an hour or two away from the feeling of wanting to stop my wheels. The Rest Stops app has been a valuable resource of information for providing me with an accurate distance from point A to B, reviews, and even photos of the actual rest area. Playlist: {Rest area reprieves and fun}

A rest stop is my first choice when I'm traveling on the interstate. You'll find stunning rest areas all over the country to provide you with a peaceful break off the road for a while. Many of them are more like gigantic parks than just a quick place to stop to stretch your legs. Tall shady trees, smooth walking paths, covered pavilion picnic areas, quaint benches, designated doggie parks, and large vending machine centers are just some of the perks you'll find, making them a welcome reprieve.

One particular rest area in Florida stands out that was very inviting and entertaining! So much so that I spent many weekends at this park—aka rest area on my days off while working in Lakeland. Sandhill cranes were roaming all around in the abundant grass areas. Standing almost four feet tall with their rattling calls were a sight and sound to behold! On the other side of the entrance was a massive herd of cows peacefully grazing in the open field. A double dose of delight!

Love's and Pilot truck stops are also a welcoming reprieve from a long day of driving or exploring. I've had fun spending a couple of bucks on a hotdog, taquito, or sausage off a roller grill during overnight stays at these places. Even though I prefer the calm ambiance of a rest area to the hustle and bustle of a truck stop, there have been times when I have thoroughly appreciated being able to stay at them.

My all-time must-stop is Buc-ee's, a Texas chain of immaculate country stores and gas stations. I love doing a slow-paced browse through their huge, inviting store and picking up a few munchies for my kids and myself. A traditional splurge each time I visit is their well-known kolache pastries. They are delectable slightly sweet bread stuffed with sausage, cheese, or both. Yum; I can't resist!

Your internet search engine is your friend when it comes to locating different rest areas and truck stops. It's as simple as asking the search engine "rest area near me" or "truck stop near me." Sometimes the search engine directions seem to be opposite of the direction I'm going (maps are not my forte), so I look on my GPS app or pay attention to road signs to see what cities are coming up near where I'm headed. I might also ask the search engine if a specific city has rest areas or truck stops near me.

{Places to park for the night} and {Continued: More cool places to sleep}

The website {Free Campsites} has also been a frequent helper when I'm not traveling down a highway. Using this site I discovered a stunning beachside spot in Montana. In addition, you can use it to locate first-class rest areas and satisfying truck stops.

Whether you fall asleep to the sound of nearby traffic, the rumbling of trucks, or the delightful sound of birds singing, I found having a variety of views and sounds to wake up to or fall asleep to each night adds to the sweetness of this life. There is joy in the hunt for a place to stop your wheels and joy in the journey.

Make today count.

Trade-Offs and Sacrifices

One of my biggest wishes in this chosen lifestyle was to live a truly serene and simple life. As the saying goes, "so far, so good." Perhaps you, too, desire to live your days or years in serenity and simplicity. I first experienced the serene and simple life by living in my car full-time for 14 months before purchasing a 2012 Toyota Highlander which I named "Happy Haven." I called my living space in my car a nest and named my living quarters in the SUV a nook.

So now you may be wondering what could be serene or simple about living in a nest or a nook, regardless of whether it is a car or SUV. To address this question, I created two lists and organized the serene and simple aspects of my preferred nomad lifestyle into two categories: (1) the serene, and (2) the simple.

Serene Living

When I first decided to live a nomadic lifestyle and embarked on this journey, I knew serenity would surround me, as I love being in nature. Find a picnic table, assemble my portable camp chair, or use a blanket to sit on, and I'm set for the day. Nomads' way of thinking is we are not living in a vehicle but rather outside our rig and this is true. I've spent more time in the great outdoors in the last three years than I have in the last two decades in a house.

Being surrounded by nature allows me to spend quiet time listening for and hearing God's voice, which is critical to my well-being and beneficial for following His will and knowing the answer to the question "what next?" It's all essential in assisting me in sorting through the pieces of important decisions I need to make and in confirming the proper direction I need to take.

One of my all-time no effort needed things to do is to look up in the sky and marvel at the stark white, velvet clouds that I simply refer to as "puffies." Like marshmallows floating above you, clouds provide instant happiness to me whether thin and wispy or bulky and lumpy. They say "everywhere you go, there you are." I say "everywhere I go, there they are!"

A continual prayer request of mine is for God to slow down my perceived tireless mind, which I refer to as the train, so I can savor the present moment. My prayer is answered in the open air, surrounded by serenity: mountains, water, trees, clouds, a sunrise, a sunset, and nature, sometimes one slice of Heaven at a time, other times all at once.

I like to refer to the landscape as God's masterpiece because it is so intricately and beautifully designed. Sometimes it requires being quiet and still, to hear the wondrous sounds of nature such as water trickling, trees blowing, and nature talking. My mind cooperates and voila—a serene and simple life. If you truly love nature, you will find beauty and serenity everywhere.

Simple Living

As I embarked on this new life, I knew there would be trade-offs and issues which would need to be figured out. Toilet, shower, microwave, refrigerator, coffee maker were all conveniences I would need or would I? They were all things I had daily access to in my former life so why wouldn't I? I would now need to figure out how to have these same accommodations, or simply do without. I looked at these items carefully one by one. Here is what I came up with:

Toilet

We all know mankind lived without the modern flush toilet for thous–ands of years. What did they do? Where did they go? The mind takes over and some of our thoughts on this subject are not pleasant. As a nomad, it is something one needs to figure out. I could see it would be another trial and error time for me. This question came up frequently on the social media groups I was a part of. It was a matter of no small concern to beginners like me.

To manage pee, I experimented with a detergent bottle and a funnel. It didn't suit my needs, so I continued to shop the aisles at various stores that carried assorted plastic containers. Nothing seemed quite right in shape or size for my comfort. Then, one day as I was strolling through the Dollar Store, I found it. A wide-mouth plastic jar.

I bought some contact paper and covered the see-through appearance of the container. This has been my go-to, or rather go-in ever since. I tuck it behind the front passenger seat and it's always handy, but out of sight. Yes, I dump appropriately and clean this necessity daily. Vinegar and water work wonders.

Probably the most universally used item for poo for nomads is a bucket. You can purchase a utility bucket in a home improvement store, line it with bags, you have an instant potty. My dilemma with this choice was where would I store this eyesore? Do I want a bucket in plain sight? The image of carrying around a big plastic bucket and constantly seeing it bothered me.

As I researched the infamous question on YouTube, I stumbled upon a lady who stored her bathroom set-up essentials (bucket, toilet paper, and bags) within the confines of a cooler. I liked this idea. Nomads always like to find at least two uses for everything we own. She doubled the use of the cooler as a seating area in her minivan.

This seemed like an unmatched solution. I found a smaller bucket and created a donut seat to fit on the rim of the bucket to use as a potty seat. I used a latex foam rubber donut-shaped seat I bought at a drugstore and had previously used as tailbone support on my desk chair when living in a house. I enlarged the seat by cutting some of the foam cushion away using a butcher knife and scissors to make the hole larger to fit the circumference of the bucket.

Since I had decided to forgo a minivan and take off in my trusty car, there was only one challenge. Where would I position this ingenious potty set-up to access it easily! I was not interested in removing any seats either.

But as God has done in so many of the details of my life, the flawless potty for me simply appeared on Amazon one day as I shopped for various fun necessities for my new life. It was a collapsible seat that folded together into a 12-inch donut in diameter and three inches in thickness. It was a perfect solution. I loved it so much that I've never looked back. It fit securely beside my pantry drawers, tucked away on the wheel hump, out of sight and out of mind. The DIY potty would not be needed after all.

Shower

The next challenge was where would I shower. Traveling all over the country, you encounter a variety of weather, with varying degrees of heat and humidity. Sometimes you wonder, "Will I ever feel clean again?" A Planet Fitness membership was usually the simple go-to answer provided when asked in the various groups. Fortunately, it is a very reasonable cost at around $20 per month, but not necessarily the ideal solution for everyone.

I gave the idea some consideration, including taking advantage of a three-day free trial pass when I first set out. I pretended to exercise then hastily ran into the shower for a much-needed rinse. I researched Planet Fitness locations and where I would ultimately be traveling.

However, they were not easily accessible in the Arizona desert, which was going to be my first stop outside of Texas. I also wasn't keen on adding expense to my very tight budget right out of the gate, or in my case, the driveway.

I researched a different option which ended up working better for me. I dropped in at the local YMCA in Texas where I was doing craft shows. They were reasonable as they used a sliding scale for low-income folk like me which was a mere $10 a month. Not only was this fee affordable but I could use my membership anywhere in the country. It fulfilled a short-term need until I headed to Quartzsite, Arizona, and the annual RTR meetup.

Once I arrived in Arizona for a 6-week stay, I found a $4 shower in an RV park I utilized a couple of times. The second year I spent in Arizona at the RTR though, the price had skyrocketed to $8. Ouch! Supply and demand had kicked in. I also met a friend who offered me a shower in their RV.

It became a non-concern once I began to discover all the places where I could access a shower inexpensively. I hit up a recreation center in Utah, then a couple of YMCAs down the road before letting go of my membership. When I started working as a camp host, I would stay clean and refreshed with baby wipes and use two small basins to wash and rinse my hair.

When I worked at Ruby's Inn, showers were provided to us. I have also rinsed off sufficiently and even washed my hair a couple of times at rest areas with private bathrooms. Once I got bold and washed my hair in the sink at a Pilot truck stop. I figured whoever was in there watching me would have a story to tell and never see me again. One of the employees came in and said, "we have showers you can use." I smiled and responded with something like "good to know." There is also a benefit to having super short hair as I was able to wash my hair in no time.

About a year into my life on the road I decided to get unintimidated, or perhaps you would call it audacious, and ask truck drivers at the truck stops if they had any spare shower credits. Someone commented on social media it was perfectly fine to ask professional drivers, as in most cases they have more showers available to them than they will ever use. A truck driver validated this comment. Knowing this provided me with the empowerment I was hoping for to feel comfortable asking the question.

When you ask and trust God with your challenges and situations, He provides you with the answers you need and will even exceed your expectations. After a year and a half of managing the "where to" shower dilemma, a very considerate person who knew me from my YouTube channel emailed me a generous gift. He happened to be a trucker who offered me the convenience of showers at the chain of truck stops where he regularly fuels. He told me about his mom's struggles as he was growing up, and this was his way of giving back to someone in need.

Knowing I was able to get a shower anytime when I was traveling the interstate was quite a blessing. I am very grateful for such a provision as this.

The bottom line is you figure it out as you go. Where you are will determine where you might find a shower. I've even showered at a hostel while visiting Zion National Park in Utah. Again, a smart tool to use is an internet search engine. Next time you're looking for a shower, ask for "showers near me."

In general, I seem to go a bit longer without showering as I feel clean and comfortable most of the time and it prevents my skin from getting dry. When I was a kid, we only bathed once a week on Saturday night before church the next day. This is also the case in my nomad life too.

Cooking

What about cooking you may ask? What would I do without a microwave to heat my favorite Lean Cuisine meals? How would I survive without a stove in those rare instances that I made a decent meal to partake of leftovers? I can assure you I had no plans of going hungry. It wasn't long before I realized I would have to give up three-minute microwave meals, as well as mucho leftovers, and replace my commonplace ways with a fresh twist.

Instead of the microwave as my go-to for something quick, now it is my one-burner Gas One brand butane/propane stove. It has replaced the four-burner traditional stove and oven for me and is my sole appliance for all my cooking needs. Soups, chili, rice, and noodle packs are now my main meals. Add a can of chicken, tuna, salmon, or ham, vegetable of your choice, and you've got a tasty casserole. It's been filling too, whether settled in at a campsite or partaking in a Hodge-podge meal at a rest area. I'm never hungry and my new quick and easy menu is endless!

Hopefully, I've eliminated microwave electromagnetic waves from my diet, which should contribute to better health for me as well. Of course, canned foods have their bad stuff and can be high in sodium, but I've discovered with this change alone I'm feeling as good as or better than when my regular go-to for dinner was using a microwave.

I'll let you in on a little secret—I never liked cooking, and some things never change. Everything is in moderation, including the consumption of canned items. I couldn't be happier, from the simplicity of a meal from a can with a two-minute heat-up time right down to the clever, compact steering wheel tray as my makeshift table which is stable, sturdy, and secure. What I call the best $10 invention ever! A simply lovely and serene life.

Refrigeration

You can't possibly live without a refrigerator, or can you? This was another of those unknowns I was determined to investigate further. What would life be without ice cream, dips, yogurt, frozen bags of vegetables, ground meat, and other staple foods? I contemplated getting a cooler to keep things iced down, or a refrigerator powered with a 12-volt plug via my Jackery, or even a house battery powered to my vehicle.

The prospect of having to deal with ice regularly was bothersome. Aside from that, figuring out how to power a refrigerator and the high cost of purchasing one didn't make me feel any better. So, I finally decided to take my small soft-sided insulated lunch bag and use it as my new mini-fridge. This is exactly what I did for the first two years of my nomad life. I tucked it on the floor in the front as far back as it would fit, the coolest part of my rig. As the saying goes, "necessity is the mother of invention," and I agree.

In this manner, I learned to limit myself to a random yogurt purchase every few weeks, a small bag of cheese sticks, mini Babybel® cheeses that can survive without refrigeration, or even a salad purchased at a discounted price from Walmart in the evening for the next day. These became my select choices for something nourishing and cold.

On occasion, I'd buy a half dozen eggs that would last me a week or more. As a side note, I understand buying eggs that haven't been washed, such as those purchased directly from a farmer, is the type of eggs you should buy if you're not going to refrigerate them. Even though it is not recommended, I have kept store-bought ones without refrigeration for extended periods. Yes, I was taking a risk, but only after researching the fact that others had done this and survived. It is entirely up to you to determine whether this is a worthy idea for you.

Of course, I've bought a few food items which later needed to be tossed. Although I loathed doing so, I justified it by knowing I had eaten at least two dollars' worth before tossing rather than purchasing a fast-food item. Those pennies and nickels add up.

Once in a while, I succumbed to and dealt with the mess of cubed ice. I'd fill up a bag or two with ice at a Subway or a similar fast-food place. Most of the time, I'd ask permission before filling up my bags from the soda fountain dispenser. Usually, the answer was yes. I would then double bag the ice and then place it inside my cooler bag on top of my items requiring refrigeration. I also took advantage of getting ice refills from the truck stop's dispenser after showering.

Earlier, I made a conscious decision to buy made-in-the-USA products, which limited my options. Around the 2-year mark of my journey, I elected to invest in an expensive cooler. It was a completely in-the-moment impulse buy, but it would provide me with easy access to more cold items which would be an upgrade. However, I ended up only using it for a short period due to its size and weight. I haven't decided whether I'll use it again or sell it.

In the interim, I came across a hot deal for a small made-in-the-USA Igloo cooler at Pro Bass where I happened to be staying overnight. Of course, I would be using ice again, but I now had a system of getting and keeping ice that was smooth and simple without the mess.

The Pro Bass deal offered $10 off your purchase if you opened a credit card account with them. It was my first credit card in nearly three years after my bankruptcy. My credit limit was $1,700 or some crazy amount like that! Here we go again. Easy credit. I said "nope" not doing it. I opened the account, made my purchase, paid it off with no interest, and then closed the account the same day. I played the game, but I didn't fall for their bait. Hallelujah!

Lastly, when I was static laboring away at Walmart for three months on two different occasions, I used the employee refrigerator not only for my lunches but also to stock up on a few frozen meals and other food. I would heat them and take them with me to eat after work in the comfort of my rig. I had a bag with my name and "do not toss" written on it. It was convenient not having to go shopping after a long day on my feet because I could go to the back, punch out for the day, grab a meal, microwave it, and go. Electromagnetic waves or not, you've got to love a microwave for quick and simple.

Coffee Maker

I admit I struggled with how to maintain my daily routine of two cups of brewed coffee. My coffee has always been very gratifying to me to kickstart my day. My first replacement for my plug-in coffee maker was a French press. I made coffee this way about two times before I arrived at the conclusion I was tired of dealing with coffee grounds every day.

Unfortunately, I tend to anoint everything with coffee, and I was sure the grounds would do the same. What's a coffee lover to do?

Next, I decided I would treat myself to a very hot cup of java from McDonald's every morning. Of course, I'd take advantage of the senior citizen discount and the free refills. After all, I was living a rent and mortgage-free life, so I could afford this little extravagance, couldn't I? Others were paying far more than $30 per month to get their fix at well-known coffee shops, so I justified my spending. I, too, needed an occasional treat or indulgence, so I made up my mind that a McDonald's coffee would be one of them.

It was all fine for about a month, and then it started bothering me. $30 per month adds up to $360 over the course of a year. Why couldn't I learn to be fond of an instant cup of coffee like my dad had done over the course of his life? The frugal side of me now kicked in.

While in my car I did not cook inside. To have boiling water, I used a 12-volt hot water pot that I plugged into the cigarette lighter. It was an efficient way to heat water when I would get up early to start traveling to my next destination. It only took about ten minutes for two cups. On days when I wasn't immediately moving on and the temperatures were near freezing, I would turn the car on and heat my water and the interior at the same time. A double dose use!

If truth be told, I took pleasure in watching the water boil on my Gas One stove. Unlike the car, I used it inside my SUV. Dipping into the instant coffee jar, adding the powder creamer, and stirring with the clanging of the spoon brought back fond memories of watching my dad make and then relax with his cup of coffee before heading out to work, or for his evening relaxation time sitting in his favorite chair. It's amazing how little things can evoke such happy thoughts. It took me a while, but I finally came to the conclusion—life is better with instant.

Air Conditioning and Heat

Okay, I'll admit I've been both very hot and extremely cold at times. The human race has survived for centuries without the use of artificial heat or air conditioning. They either warmed up in the sun or sought out shade to keep cool. At times, I simply adopted a pioneer mentality. I'd either look for places to park to satisfy my need for warmth or coolness, or I'd make a conscious decision to change my attitude toward the situation I was in. It became a simple mind-over-matter shift in thinking. Knowing and applying the adage, "this too shall pass" also helped with my shift in thinking and survival of the elements.

Layers of clothing, blankets, a beanie, gloves, and modern-day comfy wool socks (sometimes two pairs) are my go-tos for staying warm on cold days. At the RTR, someone even gave me a package of hand warmers, which I have yet to open.

In terms of staying cool on hot days, a USB-operated fan has been a lifesaver on 80-degree-plus days. Even two or three fans blowing on you can make quite a difference. In the second year of my journey, I began to put a few more handy tricks I had previously learned to use. I'd go into a fast-food restaurant, put some ice in a plastic bag, and then fill my spray bottle with ice and water for an occasional spritz. It helped immensely on those exceedingly hot days when I got off work with no plans to go anywhere. In addition to wearing lightweight clothing, fans and spritzing, I finally began using a cooling towel I had forgotten about purchasing. {Staying cool tricks}

I could only wonder why I had never used a cooling towel during my first year. Maybe it was because I hadn't figured out how to rewet it and keep it cold. One day, while at Walmart, it occurred to me that I could grab a cup of ice on my way out of work for the day, dump it in the Dollar Store plastic bowl I had purchased to wash my hair in, add water and simply re-soak the towel as needed. What a cool invention.

There were many days though when I drove long distances to avoid being stuck in the brutal heat. I was always looking ahead to see the weather forecast for the next few days so I could plan my destinations. I've also worked throughout the country while keeping the weather in mind. For example, in the winter, I was in Florida. In the late fall, I was indoors at craft shows in Texas, and in the summer, I hung out in Washington, Utah, and Montana. I've been in temperatures below freezing and temperatures above 90 degrees. No matter the temperature, God always provides. The elements of heat and cold can be our friend or foe.

As you can see, there are plenty of ways to stay comfortable without wilting or freezing to death. It all depends on whether you choose to learn and adapt. Heat and cold are unquestionably more difficult to handle than any of the other sacrifices mentioned here. It can take a lot of mental fortitude to push through the challenges. But keep in mind the weather you're experiencing now will pass. Gray skies never last.

In closing this chapter on modern conveniences and how to live with or without them, it comes down to tradeoffs. I traded some of these contemporary comforts to marvel at God's paintbrush of sunrises and sunsets every day in my "front" or "backyard." I was able to have a different setting every single day if I chose. A new place to live is a turn of the key away! My "real home" on this side of Heaven is this beautiful world, and there is something new to discover at every turn, whether on a glorious walk, in the next mile I travel, or even in a parking space for the night.

One of the most significant net results and benefits I received was genuine, heartfelt appreciation. When I shower, it feels like a special blessing, rather than something to be taken for granted. A microwave and refrigerator are luxurious conveniences to have whenever I come across them, instead of being something I couldn't live without, as it was in a house. The same can be said for my various and occasional treats and indulgences. Ice cream was something I indulged in daily. It was no longer a staple, but rather a luxury and a rare treat.

My "whys" for choosing to live this lifestyle far outweigh any heat or cold issues I might face. This life as a nomad is not about focusing on what you don't have, but rather on what you do have and the wonder and anticipation that comes with each new day. If I had to choose between this lifestyle and a shower, a refrigerator, A/C, a furnace, or even a toilet, I would choose the mammoth outdoors and pristine nature every single time. I praise God in both the storms and in the calm of my life, knowing He is with me on even the most difficult of days. "I will never leave you nor forsake you," He has stated in the Bible. This is something I firmly believe and have experienced firsthand, and my prayer is for you to experience this goodness as well.

Simple Life = Serene Life ~ Linda Mastromonaco

Solitude, Loneliness, and Isolation

Another frequently asked question I get is, "aren't you lonely in this chosen lifestyle?" My response is always the same. "No, though lonely made its presence known in sticks and bricks." It was within those four walls where lonely feelings seemed to come frequently and seemingly out of nowhere. The walls even felt like they were closing in on me at times. Not due to a lack of space, but rather from being surrounded by bittersweet memories of the past and menial stuff. A lack of company and fellowship with others made the feelings more pronounced. I was lonely, stationary.

Sure, I could go to church, volunteer, or find something to do on a Friday night to combat the loneliness. Sometimes I did, but often, I did not. It required emotional and mental energy I felt had been slowly draining from me for quite some time. I frequently lacked the energy to get dressed, look nice and leave the house.

On most days, I have the needed ambition to live my new motto GO SEE DO, which was not the case before. Now, I meet new people wherever I go. My company can be the birds singing to me in the morning, or the coyotes howling far off in the distance at night. Nature satisfies my need for the company even when no one else is around. Sometimes it's what I need to feel refreshed and whole. Every day is new and different, which alleviates the loneliness and feelings of isolation caused by the same old routine that seemed to permeate each day in my former life.

While on my journey, I've had some lengthy stays in the desert. This may sound very lonely and isolating to you. There was a time when I couldn't imagine what it would be like to spend days on end on BLM land either, with its rocky flooring, needing to be on guard of prickly plants, gusty winds, and incessant flying dust. However, what I experienced was so much more than these minor inconveniences.

The more time I spent in the desert, the more in tune everything seemed to become. Like the stillness of the desert, with all the elements coming together as if it were a song and a dance meant for each other. My senses were heightened, and I didn't have the usual distractions of everyday outdoor noises. I've been able to hear myself think, and even more profoundly, hear God whisper. The chatter in my head gets quieted, and the solace of the desert has given me opportunities to simply be still and listen.

In the desert, I made a new friend. No, not the frightening rattlesnakes and scorpions, but the desert itself has become my friend. Overall, if I had to choose between water or desert, water would be my first choice. Though being in the Arizona desert on BLM land has provided me with all the company I desired for a week, sometimes longer. This solitude is something I have chosen for myself. I'm alone but not lonely.

The desert with its expansive sandy scenery has provided me with profound silence and company, which I call "desert delight." Cactus is an incredible staple to the desert floor. You can find bright hues of purple, orange, and yellow flowers growing freely. Seeing these phenomenal desert blooms is magical. It's as if I now look forward to self-imposed isolation. I'm drawn to come back again. To me, it is serenity at its finest.

You
are the catalyst
of your
own happiness.
SIMPLE LIFE

Along with the silence and solitude of the desert, I've experienced walking through the eerily quiet rainforest in Olympic National Park, Washington, visiting the breathtaking beauty of a national or state park, which has provided me with the respite and opportunities I'd longed for. Being in these various places would quiet my restless spirit and allow me to pay attention to God's voice more clearly, leaving loneliness and isolation within four walls far behind. I never knew silence and solitude in a forest would be so delightful until I experienced it firsthand.

From the gratification of complete silence to the sound of traffic combats any lonely feelings that creep in. It's soothing white noise to me as I grew up with the constant rumblings of trucks and cars on the Pennsylvania turnpike 50 yards from my front bedroom window. On the other hand, large gatherings of people moving about, and chattering can be unsettling to me. You know, the busyness we all try to get away from when we go to the beach or the mountains for a weekend getaway during the off-season.

I've come to realize more than ever that I find satisfaction in my own company and am perfectly content sitting in my comfy camp chair, snacking, or simply having a bowl of soup. In addition, to combat loneliness I create videos of this intriguing lifestyle, then share them with the world on my YouTube channel. All the amiable comments provide virtual company too. {Serene and Simple Life}

When those rare moments of loneliness creep in, when I wish someone was around to hang out with or I had a spouse to do things with, I do my utmost to shake those feelings off and not focus on them. That's not to say I don't let my emotions in at all. On the contrary. I pay attention to my feelings, listen to them, and then let them go. My friend calls this "catch and release." It is a tool I use that you can apply if you are having negative thoughts about a situation, person, or missing someone.

Here's how it works: a thought occurs to you. For example, you think "I wish ________________ (fill in the blank with their name) would be in touch" but you can't do anything to make that happen. Feel the emotion, miss that person for a moment, then let go of the feeling dragging you down, such as loneliness, anger, sadness, or frustration. It's important not to give these thoughts power over you.

The more you become aware of these negative emotions affecting your disposition and solitude, the easier and faster you will be able to catch and release them. This is just one example of how you can use catch and release to manage your emotions.

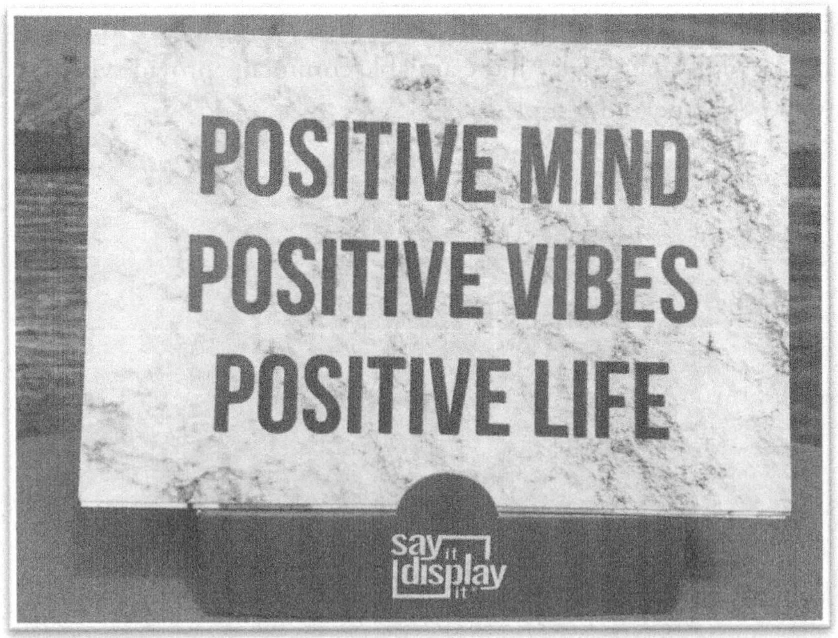

Moving from one city or state to another was an excellent antidote to loneliness which was something I did for many years. Flaming my gypsy soul and not wanting to stay anywhere for very long worked in my favor. Now, instead of major moves across the country, I head on down the road and travel to new places. It's amazing how those three little action steps GO SEE DO will affect your body, soul, and mind.

Everybody needs beauty as well as bread, places to pray in, where nature may heal and give strength to body and soul.

Friends vs. a Tribe

What is a Tribe?

Broadly defined, a tribe is a community of people who share common interests and provide support for one another. A tribe can include family members, but it is not limited to them. Our tribe may consist of friends, coworkers, neighbors, and acquaintances, among others.

Why We Need a Tribe

We are hardwired for connection from birth. When our ancestors roamed the land in search of food, moving in groups was critical to their safety and survival. To survive harsh weather and living conditions, early settlers in the United States had to rely on one another. However, as America prospered, our reliance on each other for survival dwindled.

When I became a nomad, one of my top priorities was to make new like-minded friends, like the ones I had in the direct sales industry, with whom I had been involved for many years. We shared similar interests in growing a business and the love of scrapbooking and preserving memories. We supported one another to make heirloom albums and share our passion with others.

As a nomad, I've been able to fulfill this same aspiration for a tribe of like-minded people. We bonded over our shared passion for this way of life. We also offered support to those who are considering becoming one or were new to this lifestyle. Sharing my knowledge and the gift of encouragement I possessed benefited me more than keeping it to myself. Having a tribe was a win-win for all.

I have two or three go-to friends who have known me for a long time. The best friends forever kind. They live in different parts of the country. They aren't part of my tribe. No one I've known for a long time has chosen to abandon their homestead to become a nomad, regardless of how rewarding I tell them this life is.

To be honest, I'm not sure they even have a clear understanding of what this lifestyle can offer one emotionally, mentally, physically, and spiritually. So why would they even consider a nomad life? Regardless, the true benefits of this life can only be realized when you are living it rather than reading or hearing about it.

From time to time, my stationary friends and I communicate via the old-fashioned telephone. We can be out of touch for long periods and reconnect right where we left off. When I share insights about my well-being, I can feel them nodding, though I'm not convinced they truly get it. They're probably thinking "just crazy, different Linda living a strange and unconventional life. She always was a different kind of bird."

When I've taken part in the large gathering of nomads that takes place every winter in the desert, my need for a new tribe was met. The RTR is an opportunity for people from all walks of life to participate in off-grid living with those who "get it." We say our farewells in the spring when the desert starts to heat up, repeating a common nomad phrase, "see you on down the road," which will likely be a year later. We come and go, knowing we'll reconnect at some point, somewhere.

The support, love, and care in the nomadic community are priceless. They have replaced the "back in the day" tribe I once had with a brand new one. As the old saying goes, "some friendships are meant to be for a week, some for a season, and some for a lifetime." This holds for my new tribe too!

Go make a difference. Someone needs you.

Hanging Out ~ Routine

During the RTR I was totally immersed in attending as many classes as I could on every nomad topic imaginable and asking many questions of those who were seasoned nomads. It was very easy to make many new friends. At night we would congregate around a toasty campfire, watch the dancing flames in the pitch black of the cool night air, share stories, laugh and bond with one another in ways that only a campfire can facilitate.

Before and after the RTR I was happily occupied writing my new weekly blog {Serene and Simple Life} and joining in on some good workout hikes through the dusty, parched desert with friends who had a sense of direction! Every bit of my time at the RTR and beyond was intertwined with too much fun!

When it ended, everyone was dispersing and going their separate ways. I decided to give camping a whirl for the first time by myself away from civilization. A new hang-out came highly recommended to me by a nomad acquaintance I bumped into at the laundromat. He shared a hidden gem with me to camp which I later recognized as a God wink!

The lake appeared as if by magic as I crested the ridge. No wifi, no cell service, no calendar, no clock, just the chirping of birds and the captivating beauty of the shimmery silver, giant reservoir—Lake Mead at Six Mile Cove. The opportunity to spend a few days in this tranquil environment was absolute "Heaven on earth."

{Lake Mead for a few!}

I entertained myself watching the soaring seagulls and an occasional rig driving by looking for their idyllic spot. There was a free show going on where I was entertained by very talented windsurfers. Kite flying enthusiasts provided a pleasant exhibit as they flew higher and higher, like free-spirited birds.

They say you are doing this lifestyle right if you don't have a clue what time or day of the week it is. I'm pretty certain I qualify. One day runs into the next.

My morning routine consisted of tidying up my bedding, tucking away the assorted pillows, getting dressed (in my front seat), brushing my teeth, and boiling up water for coffee. Sometimes I'd write down my plans such as where I wanted to go and what I wanted to see. On days when I chose to do nothing but breathe in the fresh air and feel the wind on my face such as in this particular setting, there was no need to write anything down! Sad days sitting alone, having a pity party where no one came were far behind me!

The majority of daylight hours were spent outdoors and the evenings tucked comfortably inside. I felt safe and secure even when I heard the high-intensity pitch of the coyotes with their yips, yaps, and loud barks. I was elated to be a visitor in their home.

It was pure joy to wake up at the crack of dawn to see the sun ascend above the horizon in the distance—a new day to celebrate being alive! Someone once said "If you want to be reminded of the love of the Lord, just watch the sunrise.

Nightfall produced a show all of its own as the sun slowly crept below the crest of the mountain. The slanting rays of the setting sun spread a warm orange hue across the sky. All of a sudden the sky was ablaze with brilliant glowing shades of red, purple, and pink. A timeless show that is always indescribably glorious.

Next, I spent another three glorious days at Stewarts Point along Lake Mead National Recreation Area in Nevada near Overton. Bumping along the rocky floor of the desert for about a mile, crawling at a snail's pace to not damage the undercarriage of my car, I found my happy spot where I would hang out some more and let the world go by. There was hardly a soul around except for a couple of Class A- RV's way in the distance.

{Stewarts Point ~ Overton, Nevada}

Alongside my camping spot, I found a flat surface to pop up my lime green shower tent used to dress in and have easy access to my collapsible potty. I was getting the hang of camping and loving it.

Reading a 200-page Christian romance novel in a day and a half was record-breaking for me. I had picked up this easy-read book at the "free" pile at the RTR. I perfected my crochet skills while staring out at the majestic beauty overlooking the lakes Northern Overton Arm. This too was a "God wink" that was shared with me at the outdoor resort I had just left!

Each day is priceless. The gift of being outdoors amongst soothing nature with no financial strain is just one of many reasons I hold fast to the fact that I am living a life of abundance—richer than I've ever been.

Be a loner. That gives you time to wonder,
to search for the truth. Have holy curiosity.
Make your life worth living.

Friendships ~ Along the Way

Aside from the tribe of friends who visit the desert each year, I've been blessed to meet and spend some quality time with a few new friends who are regular followers of my YouTube channel. They've mostly reached out to me with a simple email, then an occasional follow-up text. If we happen to be traveling in the same direction, we consider making a connection.

Having this opportunity to make connections has proven to be a beneficial way to fill the void of missing those dear to me. Friends cannot replace these special family ties, but they can help to minimize the feelings associated with being away from your immediate family and loved ones.

It's fulfilling to be surrounded by people you resonate with and who genuinely care about you. Sometimes they even become like family.

On this journey, I've been blessed several times with friends who have been there for me when I needed them. The first person I met heading to the RTR was Joan. We had been chatting back and forth on social media leading up to the Women's Rubber Tramp Rendezvous (WRTR). Eventually, we exchanged phone numbers. We decided to meet at a strip mall in Palm Springs, California to follow one another to our first gathering.

Our face-to-face meeting was at a little Mexican restaurant. We resided at a rest stop off the freeway for the night. The next day we drove into the main event together in our separate rigs. Joan's rig was a Ford Transit Connect. We set up camp near one another. Throughout the course of the WRTR and even into the RTR, we shared meals, visited a single's campfire, and randomly hung out together.

Joan has been a thoughtful friend who picks up the phone and says "hey whatcha doing lady, where are you?" She is the kind of person we all need who checks in, makes sure we're okay, and that all is well.

In December of my second year as a full-time nomad, I met Sandie in a caravan I joined. Caravans are organized groups of people who get together and camp at a specific location, and you are free to come and go whenever you want.

Sandie and I hit it off on the spot. For my YouTube channel, I interviewed a few women who were willing to share their nomad stories. After interviewing Sandie, we bonded even more. She's also funny, which makes our friendship even richer. During the interview, I kept calling her Lois. At the end of the interview, Sandie flung open the button-down shirt she had over the top of her t-shirt with her name "Sandie" on it. She smiled and said to me, "Hey Linda, it's Sandie." Too funny!

A few months after we parted ways, we reconnected via telephone. It was as if no time had passed. We caught up on life and ended our conversation by agreeing to stay in touch. {Share the love with Sandie interview}

A year later while I was working in Montana for the summer, Sandie called me out of the blue. In her caring manner, she said to me, "you've been on my heart and God gave me a nudge to call you." She expressed that she had no idea what I was doing but had a feeling I needed a break from something and extended an open invitation to come and stay on her large acreage in Washington.

A break—she had no idea how desperately I needed one. My heart raced with excitement to get a mental health break! I'd been at Walmart all summer putting in 50 hours a week in a challenging environment. As we talked, it became a huge temptation to give my two-week notice and call it a day.

Though I wanted to quit this workplace immediately, I knew I should pray about this one. The good Lord gave me the stamina to stay a little longer so I could take advantage of my employee discount, which would kick in after 90 days of employment, as well as collect my hazard bonus. Ha, ha—hazard for sure. I then submitted my notice. Thankfully, those days were finally behind me.

I took my time heading up to Washington. Two weeks to be exact and approximately 2,100 miles. First I traveled the North Unit scenic byway to visit the rugged, mysterious badlands of Theodore Roosevelt National Park in southwestern North Dakota, where I got to see enormous buffalo "up close and personal."

Next, I continued through the exhilarating states of Montana and Idaho for more captivating scenery and photos! Eventually, I arrived in Washington on Sandie's ten acres.

I hung out just chilling for the first few days, regrouping from a busy summer that had flown by way too fast. Sandie and I went on a scenic road trip and spent a few days camping for free in the unsurpassed Olympic National Forest and then moved on to a paid campground. After all, the optimum tour guide is someone who lives in and knows the area. Having companionship to sit at the fire, making new memories, and concocting some tasty meals together was a blast.

{Simple and satisfying meals}

It was my first and only time staying at a paid campground. Sandie generously picked up the tab with her state park discount card. The best part was having a like-minded company. I'm thankful for the good times which will always be etched in my heart.

Joleen and I became best buds at the same time I met Sandie. We formed our new friendship by hiking, hanging out, and chatting with one another. I also interviewed her about her "why" story for my channel. {Meet Joleen}

We parted ways from the caravan, staying in touch via text messages, commenting on each other's channels, or simply mentioning our location and travel plans. We reunited a year and a half later at a free campsite at Willow Lake, Wyoming, on national forest land. Joleen and her husband located and held a spot for me. We caught up on life and shared upbeat conversations and more good laughs.

Playlist:{Fun with Joleen Willow Lake, Wyoming}

Judy was another huge blessing that came into my life. We met at the RTR the second year I attended while we were out and about at the fairgrounds mingling with others. She introduced herself and told me she recognized me from YouTube, was an avid follower and I made her laugh. Judy shared with me that the things I say or how I comment about different things would be the exact way she would think or respond. Her expressing these sentiments was heartwarming. {Fender bender & Meet Judy! }

Little did I know what was in store for us over the next few days when God placed Judy in my path. After the RTR, I had a fender bender that needed to be repaired. While chit-chatting on the phone I mentioned my dilemma about what to do while my home was in the shop. Not knowing how I would manage or my thoughts of being without a vehicle and spending money on a motel room, Judy invited me to stay at the Airbnb she was renting for a week. Now that's what I refer to as a God send!

She was also my taxi to and from the repair shop. We did some sightseeing and hiked a bit, watched Family Feud together, and chatted about anything and everything. It was so much fun to be around someone new where you could be yourself. Not to mention the luxuries of experiencing a gorgeous Airbnb and the two lovely showers I took during this brief time of hanging out together. Perhaps one day we will reconnect where we left off.

At the end of year two and into year three on the road, I had the opportunity to meet five additional followers of Serene and Simple Life©. These encounters will forever be in my heart as some of my favorite times in this season of my life.

I casually mentioned on my channel I was looking to find somewhere with cooler temperatures in the winter to hang out for a while and go back to work. Going back to Arizona a third time did not appeal to me as I wanted to keep adding to my list of new experiences!

Kimberly from Florida emailed me. She said something like "come to Florida. I am an imperfect Christian who loves Jesus. You can park in my yard, lots of privacy." God has kept outdoing Himself with the gift of friendship and "God sends!"

We bonded almost instantaneously even with our 20-year age gap, young enough to be my daughter. Our random conversations were fulfilling and filled with much-needed humor. It's a wondrous thing to see as God uses us all for His glory. She provided homemade, hot meals after a ten-hour day at work and delivered tasty, brewed coffee right up to my car window on my days off. I guess you call that curbside service, or is that yard service? I look forward to us remaining friends for a long time to come and one day reuniting.

The four months at Kimberly's sped by. Tami emailed me during my stay. She wanted to meet and treat me to lunch. We met close by where I was staying in Florida and clicked immediately. What an awesome way to spend a day off! She invited me to visit her a couple of hours away in St. Augustine, Florida once my seasonal undertaking ended.

It was a bit too early in the year to head to Tennessee to complete my search for land for a tiny cabin. Her invitation came at the perfect time, not to mention the weather was near perfect too! We spent four days in the utmost GO SEE DO way. Tami drove us all around while I got to be the passenger! We headed downtown to the charming atmosphere of St. Augustine, dashing in and out of a ton of shops, and enjoying gourmet pizza on a bench near the waterfront. Another day was spent sitting on the windy yet beautiful, uncrowded beach overlooking the Atlantic Ocean while eating an irresistible salad, talking about everything and nothing and laughing till it hurt. We ended the day with an unfailing sunset at the magnificent pier. Playlist: {Meet Tami & St Augustine tour}

Next on the agenda—Tennessee a week later to continue pursuing a land purchase for my tiny cabin. I was on a mission. Kathy, from my channel, and I had been texting each other for many months. We connected instantly with the same Christian beliefs and our love for Jesus. We finally met at Cracker Barrel in Franklin, Tennessee, and shared a yummy meal, warm conversation, and a couple of hours exploring local shops—one of my favorite things to do! {Meet Kathy: tour her shuttle bus}

North Carolina was one of my last few states to visit before stopping in South Carolina to meet Johnette to take her up on her sweet offer from months earlier to come and stay on her private property in the woods! We also went on a GO SEE DO adventure. Upon arrival, they put me up in a luxurious hotel for the night! One of the first things I did was sit on the bed and scrolled through the TV channels with the remote like I often did in days gone by! This gesture was so unexpected and so very much appreciated. The next morning Johnette and I met for an exquisite breakfast buffet with spectacular views from the top floor.

After breakfast, we were off to have a packed day of sightseeing in Charleston, South Carolina with Johnette's daughter serving as the official tour guide. We ended our day at a popular, classy restaurant with an amazing view of the harbor from our seating.

Early one morning Johnette, her best bud, and I went to the notable Healing Springs to fill up some jugs with pure clean water. We wrapped up the day with lunch at a lovely Amish restaurant. Later in the week Johnette wanted to practice car camping, so we parked side by side by the water one night at a tiny boat dock alongside a familiar neighborhood. Too much fun—again!

Another day we strolled through fragrant-filled flower gardens, stopped by a serene park, and partook in a delicious picnic alongside a babbling brook with fresh food from a nearby grocery store. Then it was off to a popular local eatery to indulge in a mouth-watering milkshake to finish off the day. The entire week was crammed full of activity. Just the way I prefer it! The following week we took a needed break from going non-stop. I'll admit, on a couple occasions throughout my road travels, I have experienced sightseeing overload, needing to stop and regroup. Playlist: {Meet Johnette ~ her rig, sightseeing, and more}

I kicked back in the back portion of her huge acreage for another glorious week before moving on. I'm so happy and blessed to have made these new friends who share my enthusiasm for this way of life.

Following the temperatures and stretching the time in anticipation of having a landing zone, I made my way to Colorado's inviting weather where I met up with Dianna for a mini visit. We met at my YouTube channel meetup the previous year at the RTR. Her invitation came at an ideal time, as the country was starting to heat up. I resided comfortably in her driveway in her little neighborhood. She treated me to a scrumptious dinner at the Olive Garden. Going to restaurants has always been one of my favorite things to do with others, but usually pass on when I'm by myself. We explored the Red Rock amphitheater and hung out at a quaint park with lots of duck friends. Playlist: {Meet Dianna and Colorado visit}

After leaving Colorado, I went back to Sandie's a second time where I got to meet Paul, another subscriber who just happened to be a terrific Christian man. The three of us had a blast. Paul treated us to a tasty breakfast and a visit to a silly animal farm where they came right up to our window. We laughed the entire time.

{Animal farm in WA or Funny farm!}

Afterward, we headed to the heavenly Hurricane Ridge in the picturesque Olympic National Park. Lastly, we topped off our jam- packed day with a mouthwatering meal at a delightful Mexican restaurant. Best day ever! {Meet Paul!}

Never in a million years could I have imagined the new friends, blessings, and unbelievable memories I would have living this way. Priceless friendships. The gift of being a nomad keeps on giving!

Filling Voids ~ Staying Connected

Occasionally I'm asked the question, "How can you be away from your kids and grandkids? Don't you miss them?"

The bottom line is, of course, I miss my children and grandchildren. Sometimes I miss them a lot, and other times I'm out having a lively time with friends or enjoying my solitude, and I miss them in a usual way. They are always in my heart. We thoroughly enjoy our time and have a blast when we are together.

When I first became a nomad, I bought a decorative box for each of my two older grand sweet peas. I decided I would send them postcards each time I visited a new state to see where I was and could keep them in the box I had given them. I put together a small photo album of some of our joyous moments together and included one in each of their boxes. My son, daughter-in-law and littlest grand sweet pea received travel postcards from me too with lots of love attached to them.

Of course, we all know staying connected is easier than ever with technology such as video and text chats. On my journey, I made it a priority to visit my kids when I was in the vicinity and if it was convenient for them. Other times it wasn't possible to visit because of my obligations with employment in far-off states. I am thankful for the quality time we spent together and the hugs, love, and memories we shared.

On one particular occasion, I expressed my love by sending a "sunshine bucket" to them in the spring. I bought a bright yellow sand bucket and filled it with treats including markers, bubbles, and little toys for the grands. It was a lot of fun putting this gift together and sending it to them.

{Staying connected: Sunshine bucket}

Something else I do is to carry little thank you notes written by my grandkids with me to fill my heart. On my birthday, years before this nomad life came to be, they gave me a canvas tote bag personalized with their doodle art and handprints on it. Who would have known the significance of this handmade gift—years later! I take it with me when I'm out and about and put a variety of items in it like my journal or snacks. This bright-colored tote brings me smiles and glee throughout the day.

Quartzsite Municip
465
& Library

Years ago, on Mother's Day, my daughter treated me to an appetizing dinner at Disneyland. Afterwards, we went to Build-A-Bear, where we each created our stuffed bear. What fun! I named my bear "Andy" after the old hymn—"In the Garden" written by C. Austin Miles, "and He (Andy) walks with me and He talks with me, and He tells me I am His own." Andy has been my co-pilot on this journey and travel buddy! When I'm missing my family, I sometimes hug Andy a little tighter. When I look at him I'm instantly happy, recalling days gone by.

In closing, the bottom line is we are responsible for our happiness. We often look to others, including our children, to make us happy. Expecting others to make you feel good will always leave you disappointed. My very wise daughter once said to me, "I just want you to be happy." She saw I was struggling emotionally. Even though at times I have missed my children and my three adorable grandchildren, I can honestly say I am happy. Many things in life come at a cost. I'm fulfilling my daughter's wish for me, and I'm pretty certain knowing mom's happy makes her happy too.

I pray daily for my children and their immediate families. I always look forward to the next time we are together for more quality time and to make some fresh, new memories. For now, I carry on. Someone once said no expectations equal no disappointments. That seems like intelligent advice to me.

This way of life has opened new doors for me in terms of happiness, growth, and positive change. Making new friends, working for a few months in a variety of states, and traveling across the country have filled voids in my life. I am grateful and blessed.

A grateful heart is a magnet for miracles

Chapter 4

Travels Across the USA

Year One: Travels ~ Living Life Large

A significant part of my nomadic life during my first year out in the great unknown was visiting a multitude of national parks and monuments, a sprinkling of "free" state parks, and even checking out countless libraries to do computer stuff. In addition to seeing prominent sights, I also traveled many miles off the beaten path to explore places not well-known. Curiosity drove me.

Even though I always knew the world was big and there was more to GO SEE DO than anyone could accomplish in a lifetime, it never occurred to me until I became a nomad I'd see and do more in this short period than I had in my entire life.

When I let go of life as I had known it for 50-plus years, it was a slow GO. My definition of "living life large" was what I was bringing to my life in the way of new and exciting opportunities, not how I was managing without a microwave, toilet, and shower at my disposal.

The puzzle pieces began to fit together as I wrote up a rough plan on paper of where I would go and what I would do. The first three months of living full time in my car were staying within a 200-mile radius of Dallas/Fort Worth where I was participating as a vendor at craft shows which was part of my business model.

Gratitude changes everything
say it display it

FIND JOY IN THE ORDINARY
Gratitude changes everything
say it display it

Then it was off to Quartzsite, Arizona for two weeks to connect with close to 10,000 other nomads at the annual RTR meetup to learn more about this chosen lifestyle, and to make new friends who would be a new tribe of people to relate to. People from all over the country and Canada, living in cars, Class A's, and everything in between—priceless!

Playlist: {Meet ups: RTR and WRTR}

As most people are aware, Arizona attracts thousands of snowbirds during the winter due to its near-perfect temperatures while the rest of the country is freezing to death. After the meetup concluded and people started going their separate ways, I decided to stay another month to get used to my new life on BLM land. Plomosa Road in Quartzsite was a favorite hangout while spending time in Arizona. Gotta love an Arizona sunrise and sunset!

Other fun stops for a few days were Ehrenberg and Parker. {BLM land hangout in AZ} When Arizona started to heat up, I proceeded to Nevada for a few days while I waited for Utah to warm up to explore Utah's Mighty 5® National Parks. Playlist:{The Mighty 5®National Parks}

In mid-April, I visited Zion National Park in Utah for the first time. Over the next few weeks, I visited the remaining Mighty 5®, all of which were not only mighty but also magnificent. As I traveled north, I continued to check the temperatures on my weather app.

After saying adios to Utah, I toured the warmer regions of Idaho and discovered the eastern side was still in a deep freeze. The powerful Shoshone Falls is a must-see and a memory etched in my mind I will never forget. If I had only read about this gushing water source of power in a textbook, I would never have had the same comprehension or first-hand visual of this phenomenon! Nor do I think Shoshone Falls would have made any bucket list of mine. {Shoshone Falls power tour Idaho}

My planned summer destination was the Snoqualmie National Forest on the mountain loop outside of Granite Falls in Washington. There I would gain a new awareness of the ability to live life large as a camp host.

Before leaving Washington I drove to enchanting Mt. Baker then Mt. Rainier National Park. I continued to explore every single day for another two weeks before starting a new calling in Bryce Canyon City, Utah. It was off to capture some of the most prominent places in America: Glacier National Park, Montana, Grand Teton National Park, Wyoming, Rocky Mountain National Park, and Mesa Verde National Park, Colorado.

Every time I experienced gems such as these parks, I became more motivated to keep going. As impossible as it is to cover every inch of a state, I was determined to try! The goal was not to rush and miss out on the beauty but to savor it and continue to fulfill my mission to "live life large." It was a whirlwind of activity with more memories captured on my camera, etched in my heart and mind forever.

It began to dawn on me that my dream of visiting each of the 50 states before I died was becoming a realistic possibility. Temperatures were beginning to drop as I finished up my stint in Utah, so it was time to head east. Thirty-two degrees at night was enough incentive for me to get moving to reach my end destination—Acadia National Park, Maine to be enthralled by the spectacular fall colors before the deep winter freeze. It's imperative to gauge the right time for your visit before the rain and rapidly dropping temperatures move in.

The journey from Bryce City, Utah to Acadia was a mere 2700 miles. I was ecstatic about this road trip after being grounded for two months! Down the road I ventured to Iowa, Nebraska, Illinois, Indiana, and Michigan for some self-guided scenic tours. I utilize my friendly search engine for, "sightseeing near me." I also relied on some popular blogs to read up on major attractions to see and do for free in any area I was visiting.

I meandered my way through the charming state of Vermont and experienced the introduction of Fall with the finest beauty imaginable. At least at the moment! Next stop—New Hampshire as I drove to the highest peak in the Northeast, to behold the natural splendor of the rugged White Mountains with their unparalleled show of vibrant fall colors. Approximately one month after heading out from Utah I made it to my final destination, Acadia National Park! There are no words to describe this unrivaled beauty. A must-see for your bucket list.

{Made it to Acadia in time!}

I continued through the last of the five New England states—Connecticut, Rhode Island, and Massachusetts. It was a quick drive through the first two states as I soaked up more of the unending shades of fall colors in the foliage. Then on to Massachusetts to explore the historical city of Boston, which is one of the largest cities in the United States. Spending a full day of walking what felt like miles and miles through the stretched-out, busy city and meandering through the Boston Gardens was a definite highlight of the trip. I think this was the longest walking excursion I ever embarked on in a congested large city! This was another exceptional day and a true workout too! Knocking down and visiting all of the lower 48 states like bowling pins was utter fun.

As I drove along the winding roads of Tennessee and amongst the green rolling hills, the well-known Great Smoky Mountains National Park was next on my list. The rural communities of Tennessee and the small-town vibe of the state drew me in. It was as if the Lord was whispering "this is where I want you to land." I didn't know if what I heard was real, or just imagining what I wanted to hear. Maybe it was because I was in the Bible belt with an expectation of hearing from God that it was brought to my consciousness. I guess I needed to be patient and go into prayer about this preconceived notion. It was a wait and see situation. I reminded myself to wait for His perfect plan to unfold in His perfect timing, not mine.

Fall Creek Falls State Park was on my itinerary in Tennessee. All state parks in Tennessee are free to visit and immerse yourself in the surroundings. Soaking up the sights and sounds was serenity at its finest. Again, I thought I heard a whisper in my mind about a landing zone in Tennessee. It felt real yet the timing was off. There wasn't anything I was going to change about the way I was living or what I had been doing for 14 months for the foreseeable future. The bottom line is I didn't have the cash needed to purchase a landing place anywhere at this juncture in this season of my life. {Fall Creek Falls State Park, TN}

Arkansas would be the last stop on this fall road trip before heading back to the neighboring state of Texas for the craft show season, but not before visiting national park number 17–Hot Springs. I had a blast shopping in the adorable small city of Hot Springs. I splurged on a cool vintage purse and some faded washed jeans. It was my only splurge except for gifts for the grand sweet peas. Besides, buying gifts for them doesn't count as a splurge but is a necessity bringing me warmth and smiles. This state also felt like a potential landing place option but not quite like Tennessee. I couldn't shake off the feelings I had during my time there.

While in Arkansas at a truck stop, I stumbled upon what would be my next big decision. The fall season is a welcome transition of change for new knowledge and encounters!

The world is big, and I want to have a good look at it before it gets dark.

---

40 Days of Travel: Good ~ Better ~Best

Over 3000 miles were covered over six weeks—30 fun trivia facts of 40 days of travel from Utah to Maine. The entire journey is documented on my YouTube channel in the playlists.

In no particular order:

1. I spent about $700 on gas
2. My biggest splurge: $22.00 lobster roll in Cape Cod, Maine for a total of $23.45 with tax
3. Took two showers: one at a truck stop in Carlisle, Pennsylvania, the other at a YMCA in Michigan (FYI – many sink/washcloth baths)
4. Favorite state: Tennessee; runner up: Washington (though over time it reversed!)
5. Longest memorable walk: through Boston gardens and through the city itself
6. "WOW" day: Acadia National Park in Maine
7. Unbelievable fall foliage: White Mountain drive through Lincoln, New Hampshire
8. Fun shopping: Le Claire, Iowa
9. Workout, exercise, and beauty: Sleeping Bear Dunes National Lakeshore in Michigan
10. Impressive, free state park to explore: Fall Creek Falls State Park in Tennessee
11. Good times passing through Canada: the Big Apple Store
12. Colorful city to shop and walk: Gatlinburg, Tennessee
13. Prime photo ops: White Mountains, New Hampshire, Sunken Gardens, Nebraska

14. Scariest moment: at an old church with a graveyard in the Smoky Mountains at dusk and my car didn't seem to want to start up. I think it was me not turning the key far enough. Angels were watching over me as I was almost sideswiped on the interstate
15. Spookiest two hours: driving in pitch black through back roads in Maine with no rest area in sight
16. Fantastic visitor center to overnight it: Maine right off the interstate
17. Most serene bedtime spot to wake up to Lake Superior
18. God wink: Meeting Diana in Cape Cod, Massachusetts from Arlington, Texas, knew of someone selling land.
19. Coolest tour: Vermont Teddy Bear Company in Shelburne
20. Yummy fast food: truck stop – hotdog and pork egg roll (two for $3)
21. Most fun spending money: gifts for kids and grand sweet peas
22. Outstanding healthy food splurge: salad in Boston at Green Works
23. Where I spent the longest amount of time in one place: two nights and three days Walmart in Traverse, Michigan: car wash, oil change, library, shower –it was a rainy weekend
24. Least desirable time: driving through hectic Chicago around 2 p.m. with no place to park
25. Most miles in one day: 450
26. Cheap treat "win!": 35 cent mini-ice cream sandwich at a small-town gas station store
27. Crazy fact: took over 2,000 photos, many to be used in Say It Display It® products
28. Best-liked big city: Boston

29. Most interesting person I met: in Maine at a rest area – an 81-year-old man from Atlanta traveling and living in his car as he said he was following the Lord's lead in his life
30. Exuberant rainy day activity: boutique hopping & shopping in Le Claire, Iowa {Rainy day in Le Claire}

{30 fun facts of 40 days of travel}

The entire travel series: {40 Days of Travel}

Folks I encounter on this journey ask me "what is your favorite place you've visited?" I've given this question a lot of thought and consideration. The truthful answer is I don't have one except for nowhere and everywhere. What I mean is wherever I am at the moment is my favorite place! There is magnificence around every corner and every bend in the road. Kind of like chocolate, they're all my favorite.

Roads were made for journeys, not destinations ~ Confucius

National Park Journey ~ List and Links

National parks in the order I visited them (2019 - 2021)

- Joshua Tree – California
- Zion – Utah Zion National Park Zion #2 Zion #3
- Arches – Utah Arches National Park Arches #2 three hikes
- Capitol Reef – Utah Capitol Reef National Park
- Canyonlands – Utah Canyonlands Canyonlands hikes
- Bryce Canyon – Utah playlist: Bryce Canyon Adventures
- North Cascades – Washington North Cascades North Cascades #2
- Olympic – Washington Olympic National Park Marymere Falls hike
- Mt. Rainier – Washington Mt. Rainier National Park
- Glacier – Montana Glacier National Park

- Grand Tetons – Wyoming Grand Tetons National Park
- Rocky Mountains – Colorado Rocky Mountain National Park
- Mesa Verde – Colorado Mesa Verde National Park
- Indiana Dunes – Indiana
- Acadia – Maine Acadia 37 clips and Acadia forest walk
- Great Smoky Mountains – Tennessee Great Smoky Mountains National Park
- Hot Springs – Arkansas Hot Springs National Park
- Saguaro – Arizona Saguaro National Park
- Carlsbad Cavern – New Mexico Carlsbad Caverns National Park
- Big Bend – Texas Carlsbad National Park
- Theodore Roosevelt – North Dakota Theodore Roosevelt National Park
- Crater Lake – Oregon Crater Lake National Park Sunrise at Crater Lake
- Redwood – California Redwood National and State Parks

I have been to the Grand Canyon and Yellowstone National Parks while living in a house, so I did not include them in this list. They are must-sees for your bucket list too.

You are the catalyst of your happiness.

**GO SEE DO: 40 States and Canada Sightseeing ~ Free

(Except for National Parks)

States not listed here—Alaska, Delaware, Hawaii, Maryland, Minnesota, New Jersey, New York, Pennsylvania, Virginia, and West Virginia. Three of these states I have lived in and explored previously. Six of these states I visited while on vacation or business. Alaska is the last remaining state I have to explore.

Of the 40 states listed below, I have lived in four of them and revisited four of them. This was my second time in Canada.

State	Jot Down Your Sites to See
Alabama	
Bienville Square Park, Mobile	
Birmingham Botanical Gardens	
Bluff Park, Pelham	
Fallen Robot, Tuscaloosa	
Montgomery (state capital)	
Orr Park, Montevallo	
The Biggest Chair, Anniston	
Cities: Delta, Eclectic, Lineville, Millbrook, Munford, Oxford, Talladega	
Arizona	
Bill Williams Refuge	
Cibola National Wildlife Refuge	
Horseshoe Bend	
Oatman (wild donkeys)	
Saguaro National Park	
Tubac (gift stores)	
Cities: Bouse, Cottonwood, Dateland, Ehrenberg, Parker, Prescott, Quartzsite, Sedona, Yuma	
Arkansas	
Downtown Hot Springs	
Hot Springs National Park	
Ozark Mountains	
Cities: Bryant, Forrest City	
California	
Imperial Sand Dunes, Brawley	
Jedediah South Redwood State Park	
Joshua Tree National Park	
Lakepoint Park, Lake Elsinore	
Panorama Park, Panorama City	
Redwood National and State Parks	
Salvation Mountain, Slab City	
Cities: Cathedral City, Corona, Palm Springs, Whitewater	

State	Jot Down Your Sites to See
Colorado	
Garden of the Gods, Colorado Springs	
Lair O' the Bear Park, Idledale	
Lakewood: Addenbrooke, Kendrick Lake, O'Kane Parks	
Mesa Verde National Park	
Red Rock Amphitheatre, Morrison	
Rocky Mountain National Park	
Woodland Park, Colorado Springs Area	
Cities: Colorado Junction, Denver, Durango, Estes Park, Golden, Morrison, Ridgway	
Connecticut	
Elizabeth Park Rose Garden, West Hartford	
New Haven (panoramic views of coastline)	
Florida	
Destin Beach	
Fort Matanzas National Monument	
Lake Morton Historic District	
Lake Parker Park, Lakeland	
Lakeland Park	
Marineland, St. Augustine	
Old St. Augustine	
Shell Factory, North Ft. Myers	
Georgia	
Blue Ridge Mountains	
Tallulah Gorge State Park	
Idaho	
American Falls	
Craters of the Moon National Monument	
Julia Davis Park, Boise	
Kathryn Albertson Park, Boise	
Lake Hayden	
Lucky Lake Reservoir	

State	Jot Down Your Sites to See
Shoshone Falls Park, Twin Falls	
Twin Falls on Snake River, Twin Falls	
Cities: Irwin, Rine, Swan Valley	
Illinois	
North Beach, Chicago	
Starved Rock State Park, Ottawa	
Indiana	
Indiana Dunes National Park, Porter	
Turkey Run State Park, Marshall	
Iowa	
Amana Colonies	
Clear Lake City Beach and Park	
Effigy Mounds National Monument	
Field of Dreams	
Le Claire (gift stores)	
Pikes Peak State Park	
Rock Creek State Park	
World's Largest Truck Stop, Walcott	
Kansas	
Flint Hills Scenic Byway	
Geary Lake Falls, Junction City	
Gypsy Hills Scenic Drive	
Keeper of the Plains Plaza, Wichita	
Monument Rock National Landmark, Lewis	
Tallgrass Prairie National Preserve	
Wichita Veterans Memorial Park	
Cities: Albert, Bazine, Colby, Florence, Isabel, Lincolnville, Pratt, Quinter	
Kentucky	
Ark Encounter, Williamstown	
Daniel Boone National Forest	
Lake Barkley State Resort Park, Cadiz	
Cities: Hopkinsville, Horse Cave, Oak Grove, Pembroke	

State	Jot Down Your Sites to See
Louisiana	
Downtown Shreveport	
Natchitoches and Cane River Lake	
Poverty Point World Heritage Site	
Maine	
Acadia National Park: Bar Harbor, Mt. Desert, Sand Beach	
Asticou Azalea Garden	
Bass Harbor Headlight House	
Cadillac Mountain (crown jewel of North Atlantic Coast)	
Echo Lake Beach	
Piscataquis River	
Southwest Harbor	
Cities: Dennistown, Greenville, Kennebunkport, Palermo, West Forks	
Massachusetts	
Boston Public Garden	
Faneuil Hall Marketplace	
Financial District, State Street	
Harborwalk	
School State Park	
Cities: Beacon Hill, Boston Common, Cape Cod, Chatham, Rockport	
Michigan	
DH Day State Park, Glen Arbor	
Empire Bluff	
Glen Haven Historical District	
JW Wells State Park, Stephenson	
Kitchitikipi Natural Springs	
Pictured Rocks National Lakeshore	
Pierce Stocking Scenic Drive	
Sleeping Bear Dunes National Lakeshore	
South Beach Park, South Haven	
Cities: Munising, Traverse City	

State	Jot Down Your Sites to See
Mississippi	
Elvis Presley's birthplace, Tupelo	
Front Beach, Ocean Springs	
Gulf Islands National Seashore	
Jackson	
Missouri	
Alley Spring and Mill, Shannon	
Grand Falls on Shoal Creek, Joplin	
Ha Ha Tonka State Park, Camdenton	
Lake Drummonds	
Nathanael Greene Close Memorial Park	
Ozark Mountains	
Springfield Botanical Gardens	
Table Rock Lake	
Table Rock State Park	
Cities: Branson, Butler, Wright City	
Montana	
Custer Gallatin National Forest	
Flathead Lake	
Gallatin Gateway	
Glacier National Park	
Lawrence Park, Kalispell	
Marantette Park, Columbia Falls	
Cities: Big Sky, Bozeman, Helena	
Nebraska	
Car Henge, Alliance	
Carney Park, O'Neil (3 days free campsite)	
Lake McConaughy	
Scotts Bluff National Monument, Gering	
Streeter Park Campground	
Sunken Gardens, Lincoln	
Cities: Lisco, Ogallala	

Nevada	
Lake Mead National Recreation Area, on Colorado River	
Six Mile Cove, Telephone Cove, Stewart's Landing (camp free)	
Valley of Fire State Park	
New Hampshire	
Franconia Notch State Park	
Portsmouth Harbor Lighthouse	
White Mountain National Forest: Lower Falls Scenic Area, Sugar Hill Scenic Vista	
Cities: Guilford, Pittsfield, St. Albans, West Gardiner	
New Mexico	
Carlsbad Caverns National Park	
Cities: Anthony, Las Cruces,	
Deming, Lordsburg	
North Carolina	
Billy Graham's home, Eagle Lake Charlotte	
Blue Ridge Parkway	
Linville Falls	
Cities: Asheville, Barnardsville, Black Mountain, Canton, Charlotte, Horse Shoe, Marion, Newland	
North Dakota	
Rosebud	
Theodore Roosevelt National Park	
Ohio	
Catawba Island State Park	
Lakeside Marblehead	
Marblehead Lighthouse State Park	
Port Clinton	
Oklahoma	
Oklahoma City National Memorial	
State Fair Park- participated in gigantic arts and crafts fair	

Oregon	
Arch Cape	
Crater Lake National Park	
Depoe Bay	
Don and Ann Davis Park/ Lincoln County Vietnam Memorial, Newport	
Ecola State Park, Cannon Beach	
Gold Beach, Oregon Coast	
Harris Beach State Park, Brookings	
Cities: Brookings, Burns, Ft. Klamath, Harper, Juntura, Klamath Falls, Newport, Otter Rock, Riley, Ririe	
Rhode Island	
Federal Hill	
Neutaconkanut Hill Conservancy	
Newport Cliffs	
Providence Place	
South Carolina	
Angel Oak Park, Johns Island	
Barnwell State Park, Blackville	
Downtown Charleston	
Edisto Memorial Gardens, Orangeburg	
Healing Springs, Blackville	
South Dakota	
Black Hills	
Deadwood	
Sheps Canyon	
Tennessee	
Bicentennial Park, Franklin	
Downtown Gatlinburg, Knoxville, Nashville	
Fall Creek Falls State Park, Spencer	
Great Smoky Mountains National Park	
McGregor and Billy Dunlop Park, Clarksville	
Pickett CCC Memorial State Park, Jamestown	

Cities: Albany, Buffalo Valley, Cherokee, Cosby, Cumberland Furnace, Dandridge, Franklin, Holladay, Jasper, Manchester, McMinnville, Monteagle, Monticello, Newport, Paris, Pigeon Forge, Sevierville, Seymour, Smithville, South Pittsburg	
Texas	
Big Bend National Park	
Brazoria Beach County Park	
Central Park, Lewisville	
Corpus Christi	
Getzendaner Memorial Park, Waxahachie	
Magnolia Beach (camp free)	
Marfa lights, Marfa	
Old Settlers Park, Round Rock	
Padre Island	
Port Aransas	
Port Lavaca	
San Luis Island	
Schreiner Park, Junction (camp free)	
Teddy Bears Lakeside Park, Dallas	
Whitecap and Surfside beach	
Cities: Bedford, Cedar Park, Fredericksburg, Frisco, Ft. Worth, Galveston, Georgetown, Hurst, Keller, Plano, Round Rock, Salado, San Antonio Texarkana, Van, Waco	
Utah	
Cedar Breaks National Monument	
Dixie National Forest	
Mighty 5® National Parks (Arches, Bryce Canyon, Canyonlands, Capitol Reef, Zion)	
Cities: Bryce City, Moab, Springdale. St. George, Torey	

Vermont	
Ben and Jerry's Ice Cream, Waterbury	
Downtown Burlington	
Huntington Gorge	
Littleton	
Montpelier (state capital)	
Shelburne Farms	
Stowe Scenic Drive	
Vermont Teddy Bear Company, Shelburne	
Washington	
Brinnon (camp state park)	
Coupeville Lighthouse Park	
Downtown Seattle	
Ebey's Landing National Historical Reserve	
Edmonds Ferry	
Fort Casey State Park	
Mt. Baker	
Mt. Rainier National Park	
Mt. St. Helens	
Mt. Ellinor	
North Cascades National Park	
Olympic National Park: Hurricane Ridge, Marymere Falls	
Quilceda Village	
Ross Lake National Recreation Area	
San Juan Islands	
Snoqualmie National Forest	
Cities: Anaconda, Anacortes, Bellingham, Bremerton, Ellensburg, Granite Falls, Hoodsport, La Conner, Leavenworth, Mulkiteo, Naches, Port Angeles, Port Orchard, Port Townsend, Quincy, Randle, Ritzville, Seabeck, Sequim, Silverdale,	

Wisconsin	
Dekorra	
Devil's Lake State Park, Baraboo	
Milwaukee Riverwalk District	
North Point, Schlitz Park, Milwaukee	
Wyoming	
Caribou - Targhee National Forest	
Grand Tetons National Park	
Willow Lake, Pinedale (free camping)	
Cities: Buford, Cheyenne, Jackson Hole, Powell, Rock River, Rock Springs, Shoshoni	
Canada	
Big Apple Pie Store, Cramahe Colborne, Ontario	
Durham Court Park, Oshawa, Ontario	
Cities: Beachville, Clare Ontario, Oshawa	

**Many of these recommended places to see are captured on videos. Please check out the playlists of Serene and Simple Life channel for additional shows of my travels.

Travel not to find yourself but remember who you've been all along.

Chapter 5

A New Home On Wheels

Change on the Horizon

As much as I loved traveling in my reliable Acura, I was starting to have some serious thoughts that the time was drawing nearer when I may need to replace her with a newer rig. I'm not exactly sure when I started feeling this way except when I glanced at the odometer, the thoughts were more pronounced. She was climbing close to the 200,000- mile mark. Since my launch, I have added 14,000 miles to her aging body and parts. What to do, what to do?

There was a gut feeling within me this was going to be my last extended trip with Serenity. Not because she was nearing the end of her lifespan but because God had something else in mind for me as I continued.

This home for over a year has exceeded my expectations. There have been no mechanical issues or repairs. With regular oil changes and four new tires, it was a smooth ride all the way. Being super comfortable and reliable—I guess I wanted to call her "home" for just a little longer.

While in Hot Springs I mentioned stumbling upon my next "big decision." Little did I know that within five days this decision would come to fruition.

Divine Intervention ~ Again!

Late one evening in Arkansas, I found a truck stop where I could park my car and get a decent night's sleep. Since there wasn't a strong internet signal to upload or watch videos, I needed something else to do to pass the time before bed. I'd been considering looking for a newer vehicle with less mileage as the Acura was up there in years and miles! What better time than now. I wanted to check and see if any Toyota Highlanders were for sale online. My preference was to buy from a private seller. I didn't want to go through a car dealer's overpriced offerings with little knowledge of the vehicle's history other than a Carfax, which I've learned isn't always up to date or accurate.

First, I tried searching Craigslist, but for some reason I couldn't access my previous saved search, which included year(s), price range, color(s), and style. So I went over to Facebook Marketplace, as I had done a few times in the past. I had found a match for what I was looking for the previous month. I had emailed the seller, though no response. It didn't matter as I was too far away to commit to seeing it at the time.

But this time was different because I was only two days away from being back in the Dallas/Fort Worth area where I was looking. I couldn't believe what I found. "For Sale: 2012 silver Toyota Highlander" which met all my requirements (year and price), and desires (color and style) and was within 20 minutes of my Texas storage unit.

Again, I had been praying for God's will to be done for a couple of months regarding a new-to-me vehicle purchase. Was this it? I wasn't convinced I should even buy it at all, preferring instead to continue living in my car. Of course, there was no harm in exploring this listing and discovering what He may have in store next. I texted the seller almost immediately. It would happen or not if this vehicle was meant to be for me.

Daniel, the seller, contacted me early the next morning. I told him I was in Arkansas and headed back to Texas the next day. We agreed on a time to meet. It would be on a Friday and the weather forecast was calling for rain most of the weekend. This forecast would work in my favor for others not to jump on this deal. Could this be my potential vehicle? Daniel did say he had one other person interested with no official time to come by to look at the vehicle, though he was not going to wait around and hold it either. Okay, I got it. Again, my prayer was "Lord if it is your will for me then it will still be for sale when I arrive," or if not, that would be my answer as well.

I was on my way to Hot Springs National Park for the day. There were only four hours of driving back to Texas. It was starting to feel real. Would it be time to buy a new home if I liked it or even loved it? How would I know for sure? I prayed again, "Lord, show me what you would have me do. If this is the vehicle you want me to have to continue this journey and do your will, please make it clear to me. I need peace from you that only you can provide for me. Amen."

It would be the first Toyota Highlander I had ever looked at in person to consider purchasing. Would it be possible to make a decision and buy the first one I saw? Never in my life had I made a large purchase without first looking at several options. I had to ask myself, why not? If this is for me, why would I hesitate and not trust Him? If He was speaking, I needed to listen. The Lord often tries to simplify things for us, and we overthink or complicate the process.

I was sure this make of vehicle at the price he was asking wouldn't last a month, maybe not even a week. I didn't want to be one of those individuals who snoozed and lost. As I pulled up to Daniel's house, there she was. My heart raced with excitement. Was my current rig feeling a bit sad at being replaced by a shiny newer rig?

As the owner and I talked, I was overcome with emotion. I listened to his "whys" about selling and I shared my "whys" about buying. Our conversation touched my heart. The owner was a longtime Christian too, sold-out for Jesus with a tattoo on his leg saying, "Jesus freak." Was this all a dream come true or more? It felt like a heavenly appointment.

In case this was it, I moved forward with the potential purchase and scheduled a pre-buy inspection. My greatest concern was having 120,000 miles on a 2012 model, as well as being the fourth owner if I purchased the vehicle. Seemed like a lot on both fronts. The inspection passed with "very good" ratings. The Highlander would need new tires, brakes, and a transmission fluid change. Daniel gave me until 6 p.m. the same day to decide. He said I could put $100 down to hold it over the weekend. This would give me time to pray some more and contemplate a new home.

I proposed an offer of $1,000 less than his asking price over the phone earlier that day, as we were driving back to the garage where the inspection was being performed. Daniel met me halfway and lowered his price by $500. I didn't think I needed to ponder this decision all weekend though I didn't want to be hasty either. After all, except for being the fourth owner, my checklist was being met. I quickly got over the high mileage dilemma after talking in depth to the mechanics at the shop where I had the pre-inspection done. I also called a friend, gave her the low down, asked her opinion, and prayed some more.

In the parking lot after the inspection, Daniel asked me what my Christian faith meant to me. This question was totally out of the blue and off-topic! I told him Jesus is my everything and lives within me, and I am a "born-again" Christian. He instantly reduced the price by another $500 to my original offer. He said, "this will buy you new tires and the additional work that needs to be done." He told me to think about it. Daniel, with God's intervention, was making this decision much easier for me.

I called him on Monday morning and said YES! Oh my, what did I just do? There were even more things to do now. First, we went to the bank to pay off their lien with the money from the sale of the vehicle. Next, we went to the tax assessors to get temporary license plates, though it didn't happen right away as I wasn't able to reach my insurance company. Finally, we headed back to my storage unit where I rented one of their last two spaces to park my new SUV until I could drive to California and gift my car to my son.

{The big reveal}

I had previously asked him if he would like the Acura as a second vehicle when the time would come to part with her. I gave him the low down about its condition. Despite being on its second transmission, it was still running like new. However, I was not confident about continuing to travel the country in it and rolling the dice. But I was confident it was a reliable run for getting from point A to point B over short distances. {Bare bones Serenity Sedan headed to CA}

He was happy to accept my offer! I turned it over to him at 209,500 miles. Of course, Acuras have a reputation for lasting well over 300,000 miles if properly maintained which I had done. It was now up to my son to decide on any future maintenance.

Did I just buy a new home with cash? It would be the first time in my life I would not have a car payment. Only six short days had passed since the first time I saw the ad online. Now, I was the proud and joyful new owner of a 2012 Toyota Highlander.

Some opportunities only come once. Seize them.

Saving: A First for Everything

Without a doubt, God is in the details. I never imagined it would be possible to pay cash for a vehicle, let alone one less than 10 years old. That's exactly what I was able to do after being on the road full-time for 14-1/2 months and saving $8,700 in rent.

It was a profound moment. It reminded me of something a girlfriend had proclaimed to me years before. In a matter-of-fact way, she said, "God is going to restore to you what the locust has stolen." I cherished those words, considering my divorce and other struggles in my life.

My YouTube channel subscriber count and viewership had taken off. I managed two back-to-back jobs in four months in some of the country's most exquisite parts of the country. Say It Display It® launched in 2015 and was starting to pick up momentum, too, as I incorporated and shared daily inspiration on my channel.

And now here I was, handing over the money to the bank teller to pay off the seller's loan of the SUV for my brother and sister in Christ, with some additional money left over in my account. Wow! Yes, the sellers were believers. Once again the Lord had orchestrated all of it. They needed to sell things to buy a house, and I was able to save money living as a nomad so I could pay cash. They say there is a first for everything. Another first for me was to have a bank account that was healthy and thriving.

In addition, I was not desiring to put out more money to enhance my daily inspiration card business, despite having an entrepreneurial mindset, remembering how I had previously gotten caught up in the need to spend money to make money. I was elated that I was still debt free. On top of this, I was able to provide my son and daughter-in-law with a vehicle that was in good condition and also be able to keep it in the family a while longer!

I knew it was necessary to continue to watch my pennies and save my money. I didn't know at the time of this purchase what God had in mind for my future. There was a warm and fuzzy feeling within me that I didn't quite understand, believing that everything would come together when it was supposed to regarding my yearning for a landing zone. I knew that obedience and perseverance were essential.

Learn to wait on God, be still, and trust Him.
He has great plans for your life.

Why an SUV?: Differences ~ Similarities

Curiosity seekers often ask, "Why an SUV? Why not a minivan?" A minivan is what many in this lifestyle are building out for their home on wheels. I'm not and have never been a fan of minivans. Back in the day, it had the soccer mom stigma attached to it.

Oh, I had my minivan experience first-hand when I was married and had my first child. Then I wrecked it. After that it was collateral in my divorce. I guess you could say I was over the minivan adventure with sour grapes attached to it.

What about a cargo van? I considered this option while spending time at a caravan with a neighbor who pulled up by me in her Chevy Express 2500. I went so far as to ask her a million questions about it. I asked if I could sit inside her home and then imagined for a moment living in one, with extra room to work and play.

Here are my top six reasons for choosing an SUV over a cargo van:

The simplicity of my build-out. I do not need space for a cot or similar type of bed set up which means I do not need the additional space. The two middle seats were removed. Voila, a hang-out space on a rainy day when I want a change of my room view or hide out for the day.

Nook. I created a nook in the center, complete with a pale gray ottoman seat, a soft pink and gray six drawer fabric unit from the Container Store, and a petite table to set my stove on.

Windows all the way around. Even though you can have windows installed in a cargo van, it's not the same. The ability to see out front, back, left, right is more appealing to me. I spend a lot of time in my front seat working, eating, relaxing, and sleeping at night. I can see what's going on around me which I opt for. It gives me a calm, serene feeling looking out my windows all around.

Familiarity. The SUV is built on a car chassis. I was very fond of my vehicle for 17 years. To have the same kind of smooth ride is very appealing to me. The Acura was a smoother ride than the Toyota Highlander, but that's okay. I'm delighted with owning this particular type of home and the unique space it provides me over car trunk space.

Gas mileage. Yes, this is a double exclamation point. The Acura got around 30 to 35 miles to the gallon. The Toyota gets between 25 to 30 miles to the gallon. This journey has been a thrifty one to save money for my tiny cabin. I'm glad that with the amount of traveling I like to do, the amount of gas money I budget is adequate to keep my bank account in the black.

Stealthiness. I have done quite a fair amount of city dwelling. It is a feeling of being safe to blend in with all the other cars in the parking lot. No one suspects anything about my lifestyle or what I'm doing in general.

{Why an SUV and not a Van?}

Now you may be thinking that not having the ability to stand up would be a hindrance to choosing this style of rig to live in. Not so! It has a reverse effect as it pushes you to get out and do more in the long run. Isn't that one of the key motivators for choosing this way of living? It was for me! What could be deemed a negative attribute is essentially a positive one.

Years later, I'm 100% satisfied with my decision. I don't need additional space and truthfully I would go back to living in an Acura in an instant if they were affordable! Since purchasing my SUV, I've added a clam pop-up shelter to expand my living quarters when on BLM land or at campgrounds.

Everything is neat, tidy, and in its place, which is exactly the way I like it. I also have easy access to all my items without needing to shift and move things around. I can readily reach my toothbrush or a bag of chips without so much as extending an arm. My setup in the SUV provides serenity and simplicity at its finest in the same way my car did. {Up close and personal in my SUV}

For me, the SUV has fulfilled all my needs for space, comfort, and enjoyment which is why she is my "Happy Haven."

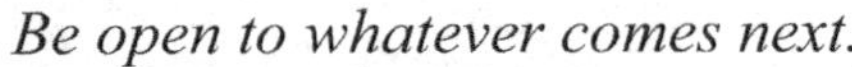

Be open to whatever comes next.

Traveling in Style: A New Home

The holiday show season in Texas had ended, and it was time to return to Arizona for my second RTR. I was looking forward to it as I was scheduled to speak on two panels that I'm quite passionate about—minimalism and stealth camping. Volunteering provided me with the opportunity to hang out with like-minded people. Volunteers were permitted to stay on the grounds of the RTR which was a bonus too.

Once the meetup ended, I needed to get my SUV bumper repaired from a previous accident. You may recall in an earlier chapter, Judy had come to my rescue as a place to stay during this repair. Next, I headed to Saguaro National Park in Arizona, with a stop in Tubac, Arizona to putz around in some very colorful shops {Shopping in Tubac, AZ} before heading to Nevada for a week camping at Telephone Cove, near Lake Mead. Then it was off for some more excitement to New Mexico's Carlsbad National Park—the third largest cave chamber in North America!

As part of my travel itinerary, I traveled back to Texas for a super fun visit with my daughter and grand sweet peas. We spent time together bowling, having lunch at one of their favorite spots, and celebrating my daughter's birthday before I headed back to a familiar park to finish out the day. Though we had gloomy weather, sunshine was abundant in my heart.

While in Texas, I spent some time at a no-frills yet overnight friendly and free city park in Junction, which had been recommended to me by a couple I met while hanging out at a caravan after the RTR. {2-day home in Junction, TX: SCORE} I also visited Marfa, Texas to see the famous mysterious Marfa lights. It was pitch black when I arrived which was a bit eerie yet made for a very restful night. {Mysterious Marfa Lights} As the weather began to warm up, I traveled to the Gulf Coast of Texas, though not before visiting a couple of state parks with my new $75 park pass. {Gulf Coast: parked on the beach!}

After leaving Texas, I made my way to Tupelo, Mississippi to see Elvis Presley's birthplace. {Elvis's birthplace} Then, off to Louisiana to see more sights recommended by Google. {Louisiana treasure} As a traveling gypsy soul, I was determined to visit the nine remaining states on the map to complete the lower 48.

There were some unexpected closures, though I did not let them deter me. I continued, passing through splendid farmland in Alabama. I made my way to Anniston, Alabama to take in more local sights and to see the biggest chair, which made the Guinness Book of World Records {Anniston, Alabama: World's biggest chair}, along with intricately designed wood tree carvings in a no-fee public park. There's so much to GO SEE DO where you don't have to spend a dime.

We must take adventures to know where we truly belong.

Chapter 6

Work While On the Road

A Digital Nomad and More

Everywhere I go, my business goes with me. I've been living life as a digital nomad with two different businesses and five online stores. It is a brilliant way to make passive income. I would never have fathomed I would be running one business while living out of a car, let alone two businesses. Bob Wells from Cheap RV Living interviewed me about how I support myself on the road. {Business in a trunk}

Online Presence

- Say It Display It® {website: }
    - {101 overview and thoughtful testimony}
    - {My business in action} playlist
- Etsy store {Say It Display It®}
- Serene and Simple Life© {My mission and purpose of the channel}
- Serene and Simple Life© products {Red Bubble}
- Serene and Simple Life© {T-Spring} (including GO SEE DO products)

SIMPLE LIFE
the moment
FAITH
over
joy in the journey
serene and simple life

SERENE and
SIMPLE LIFE
in the moment

ive in the moment
serene and simple
SERENE and
SIMPLE LIFE

Amazon Affiliate

Sharing products I use in my serene and simple life used both inside and outside my homes on wheels on my {Amazon Store}.

Your talent is God's gift to you.
What you do with it is your gift back to God.

Making a Difference ~ Fulfilling Work

"You need to start a channel," said a fellow nomad at the first RTR I attended. The thought of creating a channel made me very anxious. Opening up my car-dwelling life for the world to view felt like a pressure to perform. Knowing the devil is also in the details with his lies and attacks made me pause for half a second as I'm sure he would not want me to do something that God could use for His kingdom. In actuality, this mere fact worked in the opposite and motivated me more to consider this new idea of having a channel.

Although hesitant at first, the more I pondered the possibilities of what could come from sharing something I was so passionate about the more fun it sounded. Talking has never been a challenge so I had that going for me! After all, I began this part of my adventure for sheer fun, to be used by God, as well as an opportunity to learn to do something new and different.

I seem to gravitate towards living out of my comfort zone anyways so this would be no different. I decided to go for it no matter what the outcome would be! Right from the start, I turned it over to God to receive all the glory for what might transpire and how He may use lil ole grandma, nomad—me.

SERENE
AND
SIMPLE LIFE
New Beginnings

off the treadmill

The more videos I made, the more I wanted to do. Reading encouraging comments, helpful tips, and making new cyber friends has given me a worthwhile purpose to make a difference. For these reasons and more, I suggest you consider starting your own YouTube channel!

I considered what I would share with others in videos/shows to convey my passion as I drilled down on what my new lifestyle meant to me. I began thinking about the three most important aspects of what I wanted to accomplish on the channel. I wrote down my mission statement to focus on what I wanted to achieve.

Three-Part Mission Statement

(1) Encourage you to think about living your own serene and simple life by sharing my day-to-day journey of work, play, and travels in a car.
(2) Empower you to live a life of faith over fear.
(3) Inspire you to live in the moment with a GO SEE DO mindset.

Serene and Simple Life© Consists of Two Parts

(1) I show you how to get moving with the GO SEE DO motto by sharing:

- Walks, hikes, drives to unknown destinations. There are plaques and information boards all over—from rest areas to hikes to national parks to expand your learning.

- My travels across the awe-inspiring USA.

- ❖ Many facts, the how-tos, whats, and whys of nomad life. Check out additional links in the bonus section.

(2) I show you how to have fun in this lifestyle and on this journey:

- ❖ Being present and not taking life too seriously. Today is all we have. Make the most of it by having fun.

- ❖ Encourage you with positivity by adding Say It Display It® sayings to videos to inspire, encourage and empower you.

- ❖ Excite you with the possibilities, new blessings, new friends, life's little treasures—things I call a "SCORE."

You can take most anything I share and apply it to your own needs and wants in the way you want to live your life. You can venture into a life of serenity and simplicity living in a vehicle as a minimalist either part- or full-time. I hope that you will enjoy every day you are given. You too may be the catalyst for change in someone else's life. Life is too short to not have fun. Live a life of gratitude. God will provide.

Be bold and courageous. When you look back on your life, you'll regret the things you didn't do more than the ones you did.

"Happy Place" Offices

To keep up with my businesses and an ongoing blog, I needed to find places to hang out and get things done where there was WIFI. Picnic tables at rest areas and parks were my go-to's on nice days to function offline. I had five different offices. I love choices!

Library: There were times I spent an entire day in the library pursuing my businesses and keeping up with endless social media. On one particular occasion, I spent multiple days creating three additional Say It Display It® collections—Mighty 5®, Nomad, and Serene and Simple Life travels to expand my product line of daily inspiration cards. The Serene and Simple Life© accessories, gifts, and clothing line also came to be in libraries!

You could say the library was my home away from home, especially on frigid cold, scorching hot, or stormy days. Quite often I stayed put till they were giving us a five-minute warning over the intercom before turning the lights out. The employees were escorting me out! Back in the day, I was closing down night spots, now libraries. What a difference 30+ years can make!

Funny flashback—during some bitterly cold weather days I would run to the bathroom minutes before closing time to put on three layers of clothes before stepping out into the frigid temps to head to my car for the night. I put the heat on full blast while driving to my sleeping spot. Yes; it was frigid out but I was toasty warm with my long johns and excessive clothing!

bago

12:05

BLM land: While residing on BLM land in Arizona I set up a four-foot table with extendable legs and pulled out my laptop, battery bank, and solar panel. Voila! A "pop-up" office. The pop-up clam served as an office undercover yet outdoors too! Standing for a few hours is conducive to staying healthy. Did you know the average person sits 13 hours and sleeps 8, resulting in a sedentary lifestyle of 21 hours a day? It felt refreshing to stand and work! A definite bonus of being outdoors is solar and the sun are especially good companions. I was able to stay powered up for at least six hours and write several weekly Serene and Simple Life© blogs while off-line.

LOVE
WHAT

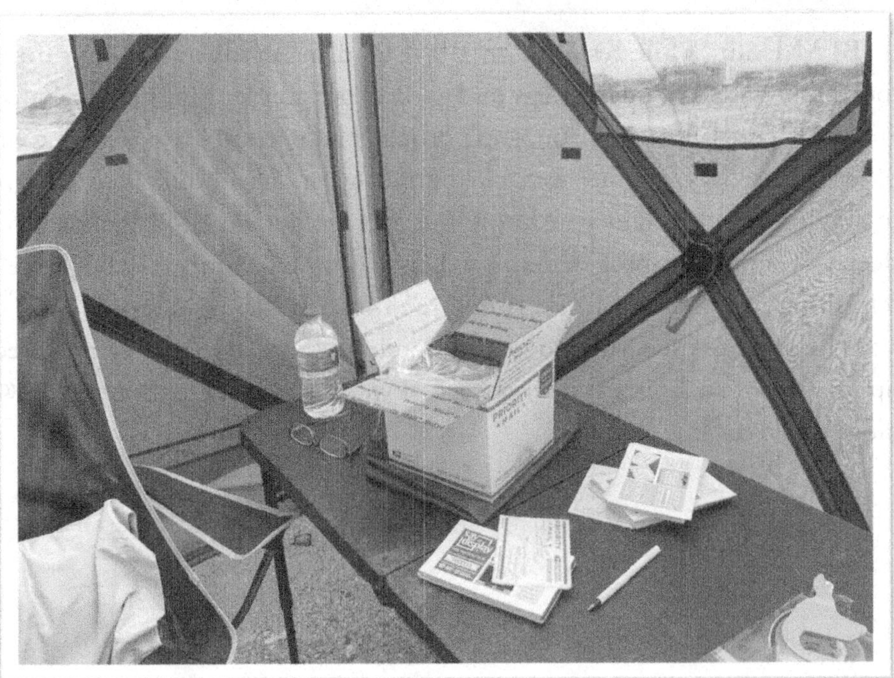
PRIORITY
MAIL

McDonald's: Another all-inclusive place to get stuff done was McDonald's. Not only because their internet is strong but because I could snack and work at the same time. Nothing like hot, greasy french fries and a thick, creamy milkshake to fuel your creativity! I liked the busy atmosphere while sitting in a spacious booth tucked way in the back. I would grab my laptop bag, notebook, highlighters, and pen and spread them out on the large tabletop. There was always an excess of tables and booths empty. Sometimes I'd be there for a couple of hours, other times a half a day, in my own little world amongst the bursts of activity of people coming and going. All-inclusive: work, eat, sightsee!

Inside car: On occasion, I did not want to go anywhere, see or talk to anyone. Especially on a gray, rainy day. My car was my "happy place" to be productive—writing, reading, and even filling orders, for many hours. I functioned in the driver's seat with the steering wheel table as my desk all the while taking in soothing views out my picture window, aka windshield. Every so often I cozied up in the nook of the SUV, hidden from the world though taking pleasure in spectacular views out the front and side windows. This activity in itself was a delightful reprieve for a while.

Picnic Table: There is something about a picnic table that makes me cheerful. I don't know if it is just a sweet memory of doing things at the picnic table at my parent's house when the kids were little. Maybe it is the many memorable picnics we had through the years or perhaps the visual of the classic, barn-red picnic table the kids and I hung out at in the backyard of our home. All the way around it was fun being together in these particular settings. I worked and lingered at many picnic tables as I traveled from one state to the next across the United States of America. Sitting outdoors and being productive on a fair weather day—it doesn't get any better than that!

Happiness cannot be far behind a grateful heart and a peaceful mind.

Year One: Seasonal Work ~ Work Is Play

In January 2019, I was hired as a camp host by California Land Management (CLM) to manage one of their four campgrounds in Washington. {Vista Recreation } I interviewed with them at the annual Big Tent event after the RTR, where hundreds of vendors from across the country sell their wares and many employers come to recruit people for summer jobs. {The Big Tent ~ Landing a summer job} Who'd have guessed this grandma would be doing life as a camp host in a deep, dark, enchanting forest in Washington! Long before the slated time of arrival, I visualized and got excited thinking about my new place to reside for a season, next to a crystal clear river and completely free. No rent!

It was mid-May when I parked my wheels at Red Bridge campground to start my job as a camp host. The campground is outside of Granite Falls on the Mt. Loop in Mt. Baker-Snoqualmie National Forest. It was a gorgeous sight to behold with 14 designated campsites along the south fork of the Stillaguamish River, nestled among the shrubs and trees.

The requirement was 25 hours per week and paid $12 per hour. I was scheduled for five consecutive days, followed by the remaining two off to do as I please. My responsibilities included checking in guests who had already reserved their campsite online, collecting camp fees in person, selling firewood, sprucing up the campsites once the site was vacated, reconciling the money collected each week with the manager, and my least pleasant duty—cleaning two pit toilets two or three times a day. Campers were always coming and going. There was always a full house.

I took great pleasure in being outdoors. Not only to save money but I was able to let go of old beliefs that I should always be doing something. Nature and the open air are great antidotes to calm your spirit.

{Camp host job series}

It was a lively time, though I had no idea this pursuit that I had been anticipating and looking forward to for months would only last a few short weeks. Though even with a looming mishap it still made the list of new and treasured experiences. I managed my own time handwriting it on a timecard, felt self-sufficient, and had no bosses hovering over me. It was unlike any other assignments I've ever had. I'd probably do it again if given the chance.

After spending eight fun-filled weeks in Washington, the mice ran me out of town, and I mean literally. They built a home in the trunk of Serenity Sedan. Ha!, no more serenity as they were going to be an ongoing challenge. In hindsight, I think God wanted to get me moving to continue the course He had put me on to have more exciting experiences!

As a result, during my first full summer season as a nomad, I would have two jobs and two completely different experiences.

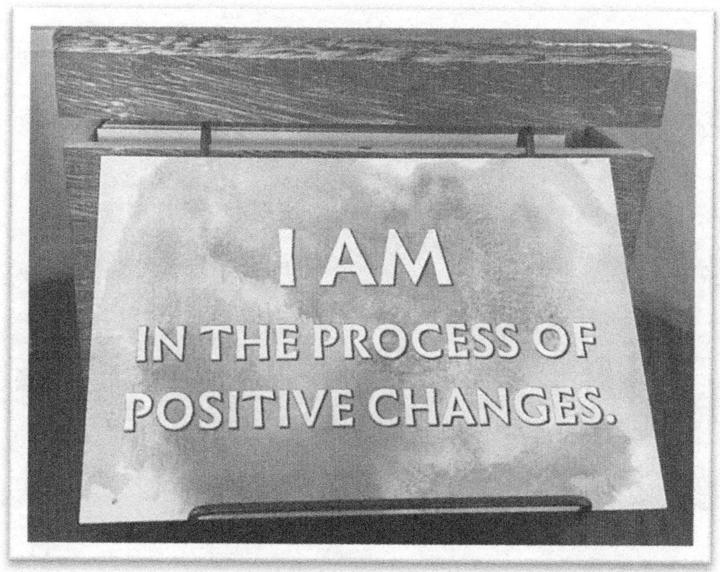

Days Off: Travels ~ Sightsee

Early afternoon on Tuesday I headed out not to return to base camp till mid-morning on Friday. This gave me an extra half a day off! My list of places to GO SEE DO in Washington was a mile long. Like one of those lists you create and can't imagine completing.

During the first four weeks, with an accumulated ten days off, I traveled thousands of miles to soak in this majestic state.

Travel Log:

Week one: Bellingham and Anacortes viewing massive amounts of boats, striking beauty, pristine waters, and serenity at its finest.

Week two: Olympic National Park with majestic snow-capped mountain peaks, black- tailed deer browsing in the huge distant fields.

Week three: Mount St. Helens active volcanic peak in the Cascade Range—learning about what transpired. Seeing the "comeback" of nature was fascinating. I gained a new appreciation for national forests with the number of operations it takes to sustain them.

Mount St. Helens – Washington
{Mount St. Helens} {Mount St. Helens #2}

Week four: North Cascades National Park with its rugged beauty, steep mountain range filled with jagged peaks, deep valleys, cascading waterfalls, and more than 300 extensive glaciers.

Local, friendly campers gave me their recommendations of additional "must sees" while in Washington. They had every sight on the list I had written out and a few others—Leavenworth, Fort Casey State Park, Whidbey Island, La Conner, Mt. Baker, and Mt Rainier. Oh my! I was bound and determined to see them all. Mission accomplished and so rewarding too!

I can see why people would claim Washington as the most beautiful state in the country. The gigantic old cedars, fragrant Douglas fir evergreens, and so many other towering trees lining sparkling lakes, massive mountains, and splendid glaciers are sights like none other.

Living in Washington as a camp host provided many opportunities to explore places that I most likely would have never seen during this lifetime. "joy in the journey" has taken on a much more significant meaning.

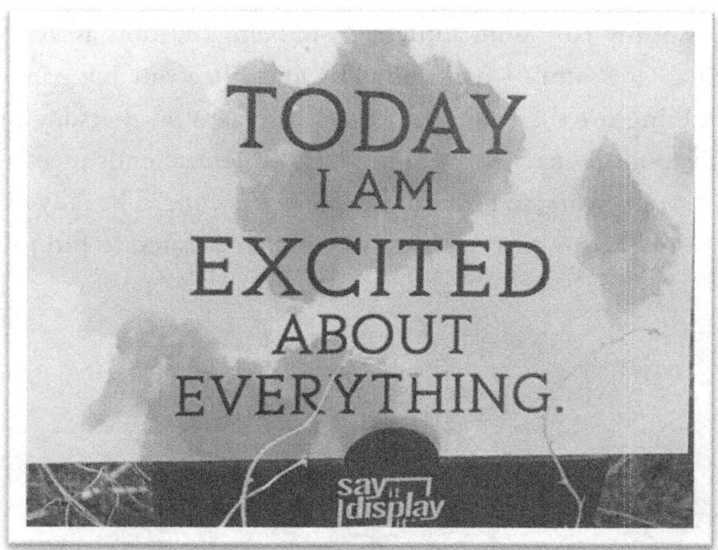

Back-Up Plan

Thankfully, when I went to the Big Tent in January to interview with a few different companies, I had a backup plan. I met with Human Resources (HR) from Ruby's Inn General Store located in Bryce Canyon City, Utah. After persuading the Board that car camping was the way of the future, they offered me a position being their very first car camper! Though it sounded great, my sense of loyalty had kicked in as I had already accepted the camp host position with CLM. Kara from Ruby's HR told me to call her if it didn't work out. I thought, okay, good to know, nice to hear but I couldn't imagine the camp host job not working out. God was preparing the way.

Now, I was on my way to Utah, 1,150 miles away from my second new experience. Though I could take my time as my upcoming manager said whenever I chose to arrive it was cool by her. This easy-going attitude and flexibility from an employer was something I'd never heard of or experienced before. After a much-needed regrouping due to the mice escapade, I traveled for two weeks through Montana, Wyoming, and Colorado, visiting the national parks well known in these states.

I arrived in Bryce Canyon City, Utah on July 15, a significant date because it was my 10-month anniversary of being full-time as a car dweller. On Monday at 9 a.m., I met with HR and filled out my paperwork. I started training for the position of sales associate on Tuesday morning. Retail and food service had been my backup "make ends meet" jobs for the past 45- plus years, so I found the job an easy one. The only difference was this would be my first no-stress job, which equated to fun to me.

The basic requirement at Ruby's was 40 hours per week. With a gorgeous mountain backdrop, brilliant sunsets every night nearby to my campsite, and friendly, amicable guests from all over the world, I had everything I needed and more. It was fascinating to meet people of different nationalities and countries. There were plenty of accents that were very pleasing to the ears. France, Germany, and Italy to name a few. I had the opportunity to work side by side with young college kids from Romania and Turkey. Yes, this grandma was continuing to accumulate those once-in-a-lifetime experiences. Playlist: {Ruby's Inn General Store job in Utah}

And the best part of all—no mice!

{My home base while working at Ruby's Inn}and {Day in the life while working at Ruby's Inn}

What a fabulous way to end the summer as I wrapped up this seasonal position mid-Sept.

Pros and Cons of Two Very Different Seasonal Jobs

Camp Host	Retail Clerk at Ruby's Inn General Store
A scenic site, next to a river, serenity at its finest	The site near restrooms and showers though not private (used by guests as well as employees
$12 an hour with a free site (2019)	$8 an hour with a $100 a month charge for a campsite. No hookups, no charge
No wifi or cell. I had to drive 17 miles for a signal. Rough on business as a digital nomad	Strong wifi and cell signal in common areas to hang out indoors.
My own boss, 25 hours a week scheduled however I chose	40 hours a week 6:45 a.m. to 2:45 p.m. to make up for the loss in pay
Isolated as a camp host. Though I made friends with campers, I was by myself most of the time	I made a couple of new friends that I was able to connect with socially a bit outside of work
No showers, 6 dollars for five minutes, 17 miles away	Showers were a one-minute walk and free
Bathroom duty with two vault toilets to clean three times a day, gross	Easy salesperson job, no bathroom duty
A uniform that consisted of men-cut pants and a dreary beige polo shirt we had to tuck in. Oh my!	Colorful t-shirt with our own jeans or shorts
Rain, rain, and more rain the first two weeks -outdoors	Rain, rain, and more rain the first two weeks -indoors
Mice	No mice

The winner: Ruby's Inn General Store, Bryce Canyon City, Utah. Moral of the story of this pros and cons list? Money isn't everything. {Camp host vs Retail clerk}

Play with a sense of urgency.

Year Two: Seasonal Work – All Over Again

My second year out would bring a completely different experience, but oh so familiar type of work. I was about to return to my first love/hate type of activity: working retail in a big chain store. What was I thinking? Or was I thinking? Initially, I had decided at the start of the year I would not get a paying job during the summer months, so I didn't attend the Big Tent event.

My decision not to pursue a paycheck came about as I talked to someone from the RTR about her experiences as a host at an RV park near Glacier National Park. She mentioned they were expanding and would most likely need help. She willingly referred me to the manager, Lisa. At first, I thought it would be cool to do something completely different and work at an RV park. In exchange for putting in ten hours a week in the main check-in office, I'd be given a space to live, reside in cooler temperatures, hike, and explore. It sounded dang near perfect!

While hanging out at Telephone Cove in Nevada, I received a call from Lisa and was hired over the phone. It was exciting to think about heading to stunning Montana for the summer and doing some more hiking in the national park. I remembered being awestruck by this magnificent park the previous summer when I road-tripped across to Montana after I left the camp host engagement in Washington. Everything seemed to be falling into place and working out.

Though at the same time, something didn't feel right about not generating any income over the summer. I was about to start receiving social security benefits, but I also needed to replenish my bank account. My thoughts about getting a tiny home or cabin had not faded either. If I was going to stay true to myself and pay cash for this next major purchase as I had planned, I knew I would need a paycheck rather than hang out in an RV park all summer without pay. I suppose you could say some common sense kicked in.

Earlier in the year, I was having a flashback when a good buddy had suggested, "you can get a job in Montana." I immediately thought to myself, "I'm not going to do that. I'm over and done with earning a couple of extra measly bucks." Though in contrast, I do find contentment in working no matter what the pay. So, it was a nagging thought as if my friend had planted a seed in my mind that I needed to work even though I didn't want to. However, I believe God uses people in our lives to help us move in the right direction if we're willing to listen.

So, I acted on the pesky thought of working retail again and called Walmart in Kalispell, Montana. I applied online, sent my resume, had a phone interview, and once again was hired immediately. As I had anticipated, the days were long, standing with exhausting hours and engaging in monotonous small talk like "hi, how's your day going" to hundreds of customers every day. I learned the Walmart in Kalispell, Montana is like three stores in one. HR had mentioned they average $300,000 in sales every day. Wow, is all I can say. One tremendous plus of being crazy busy is the days never dragged on where you get that feeling they're never going to end!

This undertaking was also 40 hours a week, full-time position. The only difference was this had been the first time in my former retail days I was able to choose my hours and days off. Maybe my retail experience carried some clout.

My schedule consisted of five days a week from 8 a.m. to 5 p.m. with Wednesday and Saturday as my days off—a Saturday off, unheard of in the retail world. I also picked up steady overtime from 5 to 7 p.m. each day. The wage was $12 per hour, plus time and a half overtime. The extra pay made me feel like I was being compensated fairly for those two additional hours each day. I put in 50 hours a week from May until the end of July. On my days off I chilled at local parks and revisited the stellar Glacier National Park.

It was imperative to pay attention to how much money I made to stay under the social security set limit. For the first time in my life, there was that possibility I would be making too much money, so I gave the standard two weeks' notice and fulfilled my 40 hours of responsibility till mid-August when I said enough! My sanity was worth more than any amount of money after a season of non-stop, monotonous work.

I think I would have gone insane at this job if it hadn't been for the great employees around me. It was quite a challenge to have a line of customers the entire shift except for two 15-minute breaks and one hour for lunch. God was stretching me, and I definitely experienced some "God growth" in terms of being tolerant and pleasant to everyone I greeted.

As it ended up, I did not take on the duties at the RV park to have a place to live. For a brief time I had considered doing both jobs. The distance from Walmart was over 30 miles, one way. Having a place to call home was going to cost me more in gas and time than I wanted to spend. Besides, I didn't want to spend so much time driving only to arrive at my site exhausted, being too tired to visit with my neighbors or do anything else.

Fortunately, I was permitted to reside in the Walmart parking lot. From the beginning, I had been upfront with my bosses. I told them I was a nomad who lived in an SUV. HR informed security of my vehicle so there would be no red flags raised that may suggest I was homeless and living there. Even though I was living there! Throughout my three and a half month stay, there were a few cars parked there day and night. Some would leave for the day but later return. They appeared to be individuals who may have been displaced in some way. Interesting though, every night, the lot had anywhere between 10 to 30 vans and RVs of various types.

Overall, staying busy in a retail environment and earning a paycheck during the hottest time of the year was a positive experience. I used to call shopping at Walmart my therapy and had been going to their stores all over the country for years to save a few dollars. Not so much anymore!

Make every day count.

Digital Nomad: Show and Go

For as long as I can remember, I've been working at art/craft fairs and shows. These types of venues have always been a source of income to help make ends meet, much like side jobs. The difference between the two was that it was a part of my business model I really enjoyed doing as my own boss. It was hit or miss as far as making a profit. They provided a way for me to keep my sanity by allowing me to spend time outdoors and interact with people, whether they were vendors, show promoters, or event attendees. There is always an instant gratification feeling that comes from having customers who are pleased with their purchase made by you.

When I first decided to become a nomad, I thought I'd call my entrepreneurial endeavors on the road "Show and Go." It sounded like it tied in with my mission of being on the move that didn't involve real labor—HA! During my first two years, I took on this feat of selling at large arts and craft shows in the Dallas/Ft Worth area from mid-September through December and even ventured out to a gigantic three-day, annual event in Oklahoma.

At the time Say It Display It® consisted of 31 different themed sets of daily inspiration cards in two different sizes. Within the confines of my car, I packed five each of the various sets in huge IKEA bags, along with (2) 4-foot tables, a narrow folding table, a backdrop display constructed with metal poles and heavy plates to mount the assembly on, plus all the needed props to show off my wares. {31 Different Themed Collections}

While situated close by to shows, I was frequently going back and forth to my storage unit to replenish products as well as picking up or dropping off my "pop-up store." I also contracted with Army Air Force Exchange Service headquarters in Dallas to sell my wares. I had an ongoing gig with them where I would work one week on, and one week off from early November through mid-December. My store was set up outside the food court and I was able to leave it intact for the entire week. My store hours were 8 am till 8 pm, seven days a week. The long hours weren't so long as it gave me something meaningful and rewarding to do. I have a simple mission statement that I'm very passionate about: changing lives one saying at a time. After many hours of educating and selling to employees and contractors coming and going, I'd head back to my vehicle for a nice, hot cup of tea, browse a little on the internet and call it a day. Get up, go, repeat!

{Aafes Show set up and in action}

Next on my itinerary was to head to AZ. I downsized my display to one table, a few props, and two bags of inventory. This was all neatly tucked in the trunk in the back of my home, commonly referred to as the garage. Everything was organized and there was no clutter or shuffling things around. I was very motivated to show and sell my Say It Display It® products in different states across the country. I also thought it would be an excellent way to grow my business.

After much consideration, I let go of the idea of doing "pop-up" shows throughout the rest of the year. I resolved not to take the risk of spending money on show fees only to break even or worse. If you're willing to pay attention, experience can be a great teacher. I also didn't want to plan my travel adventures around outdoor shows with the potential of dealing with inclement weather. It's been much more appealing to travel at a leisurely pace. As it happens, there were times that I would randomly meet someone who wanted to check out my product line. I would pop open my trunk—show and sell right from the garage!

Limiting the "work" part of my journey to pre-planned seasonal gigs made my travels much more pleasurable because there were no obligations to contend with throughout the year. Overall, besides the necessary paycheck, choosing to work turned out to be a mini reprieve from many hours behind the wheel driving throughout the country. Working was a "blessing in disguise" no matter how tedious the job was. Though after three to four months in one place I couldn't wait to get going again!

Rather than doing nothing specific to generate income from Say It Display It®, except for the unexpected sale here and there while out and about, I increased my online presence by weekly posting "Monday meaningful messages" on my Serene and Simple Life© YouTube channel. My business received a significant boost in revenue because of this action plan. Every day I was filling new orders. Free marketing, no show costs, and bigger profits. Now that's what I call smart business sense. Playlist: {Monday meaningful messages}

There are always things you can do to give your money-making ideas a boost while on the road that doesn't cost you anything but time.

One day at a time.

Chapter 7

Season of Stationary

Search for a Tiny Home Community

Since I started living this unconventional life of living in a car, one of my goals was to save enough money to purchase a shed and turn it into a cozy cabin or maybe even a tiny home on wheels. To that end, I visited a tiny home community in Texas soon after I became a nomad. When I met the owner, I shared my long-term goals of having a landing place to come back to where I could regroup, rest and refuel while continuing to feed my gypsy soul. Even though I couldn't afford to live in that community at least in the short term, it was interesting to follow them on social media.

I came across a tiny home company while browsing YouTube which seemed to offer exactly what I wanted and within my price range. Was finding this business and having them build my dream tiny cabin a result of divine intervention?

At the time, I was visiting Alabama and had planned to visit the Gulf Coast. A God-given push prompted me to call the owner of this community and ask him if I could reside on his property for a few days. In exchange, I offered to do some chores for him.

I explained to the owner I was traveling across the country and saving my money to hopefully buy one of his tiny homes. I also informed him I had sent in the required payment to hold a specific lot in one of the communities they were developing. Knowing that, he was very open, said to come by whenever, and welcomed me to stay a few.

After hanging out there for a short while, I never really experienced the peace that passes all understanding which comes from knowing this was exactly where God wanted me to secure my landing zone. Something felt off like a repeat of hasty decisions I had made in my life. I tried to convince myself it was His will for me, and therefore a worthy decision to move forward with my plans. I wanted the same sense of assurance I had experienced when I purchased the SUV which told me I was in line with His plan for my life. But it wasn't there.

Maybe it was time to move on and give some more thought to this potential community I would call home. So, I headed to Montana to work to save more money to fulfill my dream. I kept thinking about moving to this community, my mind racing with the pros, cons and everything in between.

One day in the break room the peace I was looking for came to me. I needed to scratch my plans for a tiny home build there and request a refund of my deposit which I quickly received once they filled the lot. The saying "all's well that ends well," came to me as it opened the door for someone else but now what was I going to do?

I'm thankful I had the opportunity to stay in that community to come to terms with what I wanted and didn't want and take more time to see what new doors the Lord would open for me. If I hadn't halted my travels for those few weeks, I might have moved forward with this initial "Plan A" and made a decision I would later regret.

God really does work in mysterious ways and has taken me to places where certain instances occurred or showed me things firsthand that I needed to pay attention to—to possibly change course. This direct encounter reminded me of how He gradually transforms negative events and circumstances into positive ones. I was reminded that important life decisions turn out far better when they are done in His time, not ours.

In retrospect, I believe I was being shielded from something He alone knew would not satisfy my heart's desires. I'm confident God provided this opportunity to show me the direction He ultimately wanted me to go to find a landing zone. If we thirst for God's will and direction, we must ask Him and pay attention when He speaks.

Hold on. God knows what He is doing.

A Different Plan ~ Shed to Cabin

As I continued to stay plugged into social media I stumbled upon a comment about a woman who owned property close to where I had recently stayed. She was planning to develop her 41 acres into a tiny home community.

One Saturday morning while I was off playing I called the landowner of this new find. We had a delightful conversation and I instantly connected with this sweet, feisty, elderly lady with lofty dreams and goals of her own. She said I could lease a lot from her and recommended a company that does exceptional craftsmanship in building out sheds into cabins. I promptly scribbled down the number, though I continued to reflect on what God had in mind for me with the many built-out tiny homes on wheels I had seen in my travels.

I shifted my thinking and began picturing a shed converted into a cabin. If I chose this path, I would be returning to the ideas I had when I first began my nomadic journey. I even made an early stop on my journey to look at sheds. {Thinking ahead: She sheds! First look on journey} After initially looking at one company, I later moved on to explore a few more. {More "shed-to-cabin " finds}

There was a chance I would be getting more bang for my buck with a bigger home by going the shed route with what I could afford. This new idea excited me. To be honest, I get excited at almost everything. Is that a squirrel outside my window? I'm excited!

The first step in this new venture was to contact the recommended company. I felt an even stronger urge to delve deeper into this new shed to cabin concept, with affordability at the forefront of my mind. I called their number and found them to be very professional. I could also tell by their customer service and attention to detail this company was exactly what I was looking for. God was giving me the attention to detail I craved, though not so fast.

The shed-to-cabin idea was slowed down because I had to wait for the landowner to give me the go ahead. She mentioned in our initial conversation that she hoped to initially develop five lots with septic systems, but was waiting on approval from the county. Unfortunately, they squelched her plan as only three tiny homes would be permitted in this particular area. I was disappointed knowing she had already filled the available lots. The newly opened door I was so excited about was rapidly closing. I couldn't help but ask God, "what is going on?"

I've had enough life experiences to know if God does not grant us our wishes, it is because He has something even better planned for us. At that moment though, I could not fathom what could be better than a spacious shed built into a cabin tucked away in the woods with only a few neighbors living around me. Once more, I had to put my faith in His plan to provide for my needs and get back to being a full-time nomad until He revealed where I should go next.

The landowner kept my phone number to give me updates as her plans progressed. A few weeks later I received a call from her to tell me she quite possibly had a lot coming available in a few months on the top of a hill. It sounded perfect! Interestingly enough, the builder I had conversed with was familiar with the layout of her land and had casually commented about this lot as an ideal location. With a babbling brook below the property, I envisioned this setting as a little slice of heaven. Oh my, had God once again exceeded my expectations during this two-year nomadic journey? Hmmm...not so fast.

It was a period of uncertainty as to whether this was the plan God had chosen for me. No doubt, I was given these circumstances to increase my faith, trust, and patience. Sadly, patience has never been one of my better virtues, but that was no surprise to God. He was building my faith muscles!

Sometimes my plans fail,
but God always gives me a better option.

Year Three: Decisions ~ Changes ~ Desires

Early in September 2020, I left Kalispell, Montana. It was still too hot to return to Texas to fulfill about a dozen back orders I received during the summer. What to do next and where to go was a pressing concern to figure out!

In my second year of attending the RTR, I met Sandie, who I introduced you to in the chapter on friends. She called me out of the blue and invited me to her newly inherited property in Washington state.

I accepted her offer to get a much-needed break from the demands and stresses of my summer escapade and to spend a couple of weeks with a friend in another "near perfect" weather state— Washington. It was with tremendous cheer to return to one of my most admired states.

As I slowly made my way to Washington, I continued to contemplate the potential lot my friend had called me about. She was a very young "80 something," but for the life of her, she could not comprehend my living and thriving in an SUV. She would randomly call me and ask, "where are you now?" She'd laugh no matter where I told her I was, and she always ended our calls with "now you be safe out there Linda." It was precious to have someone like her checking in with me.

While back in Washington I learned there were new complications with the county regarding putting a shed-to-cabin on her land. As it turns out, I would need to have the cabin finished before moving it onto the lot, but the builder I had been pursuing no longer performed electrical or plumbing work on-site. The situation became overly complicated due to not having a lot secured, the county's rules, etc. Like the tiny home community I had to walk away from, I accepted this too was not meant to be.

During the next two weeks, Sandie and I camped, dined out, ran errands, and went sightseeing. I made plans to head back to Tennessee after the necessary stop in Texas to fill some orders. I completely let go of the idea of leasing land in a community. I concluded the ultimate plan for me would be to look for a half-acre to an acre of land to do as I please. I was going to be a landowner. Not so fast.

I called a realtor who had been recommended to me and made an appointment to meet once I made a quick visit back to Texas. She was certain she could find me a piece of land that would meet all my criteria:

- Not too remote—a few outlying neighbors
- $30,000 budget which would include water and septic
- Not on a hill where cutting a steep driveway would be a challenge
- Not a forest of trees that would require major excavation
- Unrestricted land for a tiny cabin

{Unrestricted land: top 10 considerations}

I came to terms with the realization I had no desire to lease land in the grand scheme of things. As I had done for most of my life, it felt as though I would be wasting money. I had no idea what I would discover or where this journey to a landing zone would take me over the next six months.

Trust the wait. Embrace the uncertainties.

A New Season: Buying Land

The search for a small plot of land began. It has never been in my nature to take things slowly once an idea has occurred to me. This would not be any different. Over the course of two weeks, I looked at 33 plots, made countless phone calls, met with a couple of different realtors, and searched online at all hours of the day and night. I've always done things with a sense of urgency, and this was no exception.

My land search journey took me from east to middle Tennessee. Within a short time, the cost of land and the prepping required to make it livable began to feel like a daunting, unrealistic dream. I pushed through my negative emotions. I forged ahead with certainty and conviction because I felt I was being directed to proceed.

Along with the steps I took to find a small piece of land, there were a couple of other instances of an Almighty intervention. One evening, I met a congenial couple while in an area I assumed had unrestricted plots for sale. It turned out to be a suburb with million-dollar homes. Oops! As I often did, I was photographing a heavenly sunset after an exhausting day, when they pulled up. We chatted for a while before discovering he was a land buyer and seller.

He shared with me an idea he was contemplating, developing an RV park. In addition, someone had donated a huge cross to place on his land. He showed me a photo of it he had taken on his phone. He also casually mentioned he could picture my tiny cabin facing the cross, so I could see it every day. "Really Lord," I silently thought. After an exhausting week of what felt like dead ends and closed doors on this power search for land, my hopes soared.

The second divine intervention moment occurred when I called a county planning commission to ask about building restrictions of a lot I had found online. I was given the name and phone number of a realtor who had developed land in the surrounding area I was interested in. They said he would know more about the restrictions in that area. I learned there were plenty of them where this lot was located! The realtor then informed me he owned some wooded property near a lake and was considering cutting and selling it for a few tiny cabins. Could this be it?

Even though I was unable to secure a land purchase during this 2-week period, I felt comfort knowing everything was coming to fruition as planned. The only real roadblock was a lack of funds to be true to myself to pay cash or go without. While settling in for the night inside my SUV, I would often review my financials on paper. It seemed like this was going to be a miracle stretch to meet my preferred objective to pay cash for both a piece of land and a tiny cabin. But God is in the business of performing miracles.

Because I was already in the Walmart system, I decided to keep things simple and return there in the fall of 2020 to make a little extra money. Hopefully, this would bring my dream of paying cash for both a tiny cabin and land to fruition. It didn't take me long to decide on Florida as a place to find employment because it's one of the few states where you can survive winter while living in a vehicle. However, I had no idea where exactly that would be nor where I would park my home during the holiday season.

Within a few days, I received an email from my buddy Kimberly who I introduced to you earlier. She lived in Florida and told me I was welcome to park on her property anytime. She welcomed me with open arms like Jesus Himself would do.

The interactions I had with the two landowners both happened to be Christians, which made me even more hopeful of a divine plan. Surely one of them would be the answer to my prayer. As it turned out, they were both in the early stages of their ideas.

I was confident God was toiling behind the scenes, and once I completed another seasonal challenge, everything was going to fall in place.

Faith and expectancy go together.

[24 Part Series: Looking for land}

Picking Up Where I Left Off ~ Now What?

The time passed by in a flash in Florida. Again, I worked for three and a half months, as an online grocery picker though I also cashiered like before to pick up extra hours. {Walmart Jobs: Cashier vs Online Picker} I kept my sanity due to the safe place to park that Kimberly provided me each night after another long, hard day to settle in for the night.

On one of my days off, I drove to the Shell Factory to shop for my grand sweet peas' Christmas presents. {Shell Factory Fun} I was always fond of exploring the stunning parks close by where I would go on walks, relax and regroup to prepare for another day on the job in less-than-ideal conditions. {Florida Day Trip to beaches}

After I quit this "nine to five", I traveled to St. Augustine to hang out with another sweet friend, Tami, mentioned before. Once more, it was a delightful respite before returning to the land search with vigor. I started by following up with my two new leads from earlier. Unfortunately, they had no exciting concrete information to share. Those doors also appeared to be slowly closing.

I returned to Tennessee in March 2021. I told myself this time it was going to be different. I was bound and determined to not drag out the search looking at countless pieces of land. I was committed to locating the piece of land meant for me. This time around, I only looked at 11 plots compared to more than 30 the first time.

I was mentally exhausted. A few days later in the evening, I returned to the first plot I had looked at during this second time around land search. Of the 11 plots, this was the only one that even remotely interested me. I was determined to complete the task of looking for land to purchase and have a successful outcome!

Revisiting this plot was a huge awakening for me. The property I was considering didn't feel at all like where I would want my landing zone to be. It was eerily quiet, surrounded by a few dilapidated sheds, and not far away was an abandoned, rundown vacant shack for sale. What was I thinking? Was I trying to talk myself into purchasing something, anything because so many doors had shut behind me? It was time to delve more deeply into what was being revealed to me and what I yearned for. It was obvious the time had come to slow up this land-buying mission.

"God, if it is your will for me to wait to buy land, then so be it," was my prayer. Next, I would head back to Texas to fill another backlog of orders as I had in the fall. I figured I would put my land search on the shelf for a while, but that was not the case.

After searching a second time in Tennessee for land, I asked God, "now what?" Funny how sometimes He responds immediately and sometimes He takes a lot longer than you anticipate. As I was looking through my mess of scribbled notes, I found a website for a place someone had recommended the previous year. No—It couldn't possibly be He wanted me to go look at another community with leased lots! What do they say about the third time's a charm?

I reasoned I had nothing to lose by checking out this random place on my way back to the great state of Texas. It would provide me with additional things to consider during another long road trip. The next day, determined to leave no stone unturned, I set out to investigate. It was a very different feeling from the first community I had looked at a year earlier. Was this happening or had I entered the twilight zone? It was late in the afternoon on a beautiful day.

I met the owner and we drove a distance to reach the community. As I was following him, I was trying to grasp exactly what I was doing! A warm fuzzy feeling came over me. Suddenly, God quietly spoke in my soul, and I listened. The decision was made. I gave a check to him for the required $1,000 down payment to hold a lot.

It was a new beginning moment, a new day, and a new opportunity to have a landing zone. Not only that but it was a small community on three-quarters of an acre with a resort-style pool and much more. The highlight being that it was tucked away in the woods with an impressive view of the mountains.

Seemingly I needed to be taken down a long and winding road, both figuratively and literally, for me to see the unparalleled gift the Lord had chosen for me. It was uncertain to me how long this chapter of my life would be as I still believe there is a piece of dirt with my name on it somewhere; for me to call my own. This feels like a stepping stone I accept in gratitude as He prepares me for even something better in the future.

Years ago, a business associate gave me a miniature, free-standing plaque with a scripture verse printed on it in gold script on a black background that said, "Delight thyself also in the Lord, and He shall give thee the desires of thine heart." (Psalms 37:4) Everywhere I've lived this plaque has been displayed. Mom had given me a colorful saying on a stand "One day at a time." Both of these messages correspond to what God has been doing and showing me. When I came to the ultimate decision to lease instead of purchase land, I felt certain that my finances will be in a better position so one day I can pay cash for that dirt!

Now that I had a location for my tiny cabin, it was time to get busy figuring out where this tiny home was going to come from. Would I have a shed built out or would I hire a tiny cabin builder? The type of tiny home had to be approved by the owner of the land. A shed-to-cabin was not acceptable so the decision was easy!

As it turned out, after I returned to Texas in early Spring for a visit, I headed back to Tennessee to once again look into Hilltop Structures, a Mennonite builder, which had been referred to me. {First look at Hilltop Structures} Knowing their reputation for quality craftsmanship made them an easy choice. The decision was made!

Besides, when all is said and done, you can be spending the same amount of money to contract others to finish out a shell. If you are handy or have friends who are, then that may be another option for you to consider. I liked having a structure built to RVIA codes so it could be easily sold or moved to another location if desired. I especially like when God simplifies matters for us and makes the path clear.

God is never early. He is never late.
God is always right on time.

**Year Three: Travels Resume ~ Highlights!

The tiny cabin was ordered. It felt surreal. They were around six to eight months out with their build schedule which meant I had a lot of time on my hands to continue my GO SEE DO adventure. Actually, the allotted time would be just right to achieve my goal of visiting all of the **lower 48 states. The only challenge I foresaw was knowing that the country would be heating up very soon. It would be a small window of time to hit up the five remaining states while cooler temperatures still abounded before reaching the sixth and final state.

Throughout my time on the road, I have always looked ahead to follow the cooler temperatures, especially for sleeping. Fans meet the demand but 80s at night makes physical comfort just a bit harder to manage.

The first state on the remaining list—North Carolina. It was once again those "near perfect" 70-degree temperatures as I traveled on the sensational Blue Ridge Parkway and checked out some of the recommended highlights. Then onto charming South Carolina to meet up with Johnette for some awesome adventures. Within two weeks temperatures were on the rise.

Arc Encounter, a huge five-story museum representation of Noah's Ark in Williamstown, Kentucky was next up. What a treasure this was to visit! It is a one-of-a-kind wonder, and the only attraction I paid an entrance fee to see in over three years!

Onward—to state numbers four and five. Missouri was lovely, much more so than I ever imagined. I spent hours meandering through Nathanael Greene Close Memorial Park; free! There was so much to see with an abundance of fragrant flower gardens articulately designed and sprawled throughout the well-manicured, lush green walkway. I snapped a boatload of pictures, some from a distance and others up close like the dainty, delicate, flowers in an array of dazzling, brilliant colors. Flowers add a touch of beauty wherever they are and make you smile. There is something special about flowers and they make people happy. I know they do me!

Next stop, next door—Kansas. The land of Dorothy in *The Wizard of Oz* and so much more! The temps were rising but I was determined to see everything I could while the heat was still bearable. I really enjoyed driving through the vast, pampered farmlands that seemed to expand into eternity. It was near nightfall when I entered Monument Rocks and Chalk Pyramids. What a sight to see—70 feet-tall sedimentary formations formed 80 million years ago!

Out of the extreme heat, I moved into a desirable climate in Colorado Springs, for a mini stay. It was sheer delight to encounter new places that I had not visited two years prior when I was in the state. Garden of the Gods made my favorites list. It is a natural landmark nestled at the foot of Pikes Peak. I slowly wandered the windy trails to witness massive red rocks sticking straight out of the ground. The serene and relaxing moments here will be noted forever. I stopped to see Dianna in Denver for a few. Read more about friends mentioned here in chapter 3.

{Garden of the Gods splendor ~Colorado}

Where can one go to escape the heat in the summer! It was the beginning of July and choices for cooler weather were getting slimmer. Looking back, I had spent the last two summers working in Washington, Utah, and Montana to survive the soaring temperatures. This was my first summer hanging out with no definitive schedule, providing me the extra time to be able to accomplish my "lower 48" mission! Wyoming was the "cooler weather" answer, though barely! One of my all-time simple pleasures was watching the very active, playful Prairie dogs at a rest area in Cheyenne. They are known as "cousins of squirrels." I adore squirrels with their long, bushy tails and at times feel like I'm one myself—scampering to and fro, never staying in one place very long! Prairie dogs have lots of cuteness with their short muscular legs, miniature rounded ears, and mini tails. Seeing them darting in and out of their burrow mounds, staring straight at you while standing on their two hind legs was a blast. It doesn't take much to get me excited!

{Prairie Dog Town}

Joleen and I spent a few days catching up at peaceful Willow Lake on the outskirts of Pinedale before it was time to move on again to my final visit of the lower 48–Oregon! {Heading into Willow Lake, Wyoming at sunset}

Just when I thought I couldn't possibly see any beauty to top what I'd already experienced, Oregon shows up! What do they say about saving the best for last? I don't know if this was the Almighty's plan or not but it sorta felt that way. Yes, the Oregon Coast, is a world unto itself with its awe-inspiring beauty. Boasting 363 miles of rugged shoreline, hidden coves, and impossibly gorgeous panoramas, the Oregon coast captivates and inspires!

I fell in love with the coastal culture and the quaint, waterfront towns as I knew I would. A few nights were spent making memories at the remarkable Depoe Bay with its rugged rocky coastline and snug harbor, spectacular coastal views at Gold Beach rest area, and the exceptional town of Newport beside the crystal clear ocean. My most beloved place to be is waking up to the glorious sunrise, the cooling, gentle breeze, and the sound of the mighty waves crashing onto the beach. Check! {Newport, Oregon ~ meet a local! }

No matter where it may be, the ocean always gives me the feeling of being relaxed and satisfied. What is it about a walk on the beach that is so invigorating? I read somewhere that the negative ions (oxygen ions with an extra electron attached, produced via water molecules) in the ocean air can calm your brain. Negative ions have been shown to have a pronounced anti-depressant effect as well. Science sense you could say.

Feeling the cool breeze on your face, smelling the saltiness of the sea, hearing the cries of the seagulls, and seeing the waves oozing onto the beach are all entrancing. My "sense" is that the beach and the ocean captivate all my senses, providing a helpful anti-depressant too. {Living at the Ocean on Oregon Coast}

Now it is not possible to visit Oregon without stopping by to see Crater Lake National Park. Oh my gosh is all I can say! It is the deepest lake in America and is famous for its intensely blue color. Furthermore, it is a natural wonder born out of violent eruptions of spitting fire and rocks—a cataclysmic volcanic eruption. I spent one evening watching the magical spectacle of nature as the sun departed then got up early the next morning to chase a breathtaking sunrise as the sun climbed over the ridge, slowly illuminating the landscape with yellow and oranges. When you visit Crater Lake National Park expect solitude and grandiose scenery, nothing less.

{Sunset at Crater Lake}
{Up with the Sunrise at Crater Lake}

In between various explorations in Oregon, I couldn't bypass Redwood National and State Parks in the northernmost coastal CA. It was another extraordinary time of capturing beauty like none other. From the spectacular giant sequoia trees that can live to be 2000 years old and grow to over 300 feet tall to spruce, hemlock, and Douglas fir—all magnificent trees in their own right, make for quite a scene! It was eerily quiet as I drove and walked through old-growth forests. I loved every minute of this occasion. The fresh tree smells were intoxicating.

{Stroll through Redwoods National Park, California}

It was too early to halt my travels so I headed to Washington for one last look. Sandie invited me back to her property. It was refreshing to stay put for a few as it was unusually hot everywhere in the country except for the higher elevations or the coast. Within a couple of weeks, I said my farewells to catch a glimpse of a few more sights a second time around. Driving through the outskirts of Yellowstone and soaking up some more scenery in Montana ended my out west excursions—for now. What a stellar way to wrap up this time! Hard to believe it had been a year since I was in this state slaving away at that big box store.

{Big Sky Montana!}

Five months flew by in no time. Three years of sweet bliss went by even faster. It was time to say goodbye to some of my most cherished moments on this fabulous journey of a lifetime. I turned around to head east. The build of my cabin was about to begin! As always, I didn't want to miss this monumental moment. Step by step I planned to video the progress of my tiny home build, and create an extraordinary series for my channel! {Cabin build series}

With a little additional time to kill I wanted to revisit the recently cleared lot where my new home was going to be. This would give me a chance to discuss with the owner the positioning of my cabin for the million dollar view and the exact placement of the septic system.

Out of the blue, I received a call from the dear lady about her land endeavor. Her latest news was the lot on the hill she had called me about months before was now ready to be occupied. Oh my, was the devil who is the author of confusion trying to taunt me? I had already moved on and now this news! Curiosity got the best of me. I was intrigued as the lot lease would be half the amount I was going to be paying.

No harm in looking—so I made the trip. After all, I had never even met her in person nor seen her tiny home village project except in photos. As I expected it was on a hill, but unfortunately there was no babbling brook below. Furthermore, it was a rough ride in and fairly remote. God had just given me a double dose of validation! The decision to live where I was initially headed before this little detour had His full endorsement and stamp of approval. In two short months, I would be experiencing a new season on my journey as I turned the page of this chapter to the next.

If I hadn't taken the time to see this lot firsthand I would have never known and maybe even wondered later if I made the right decision. The perfect peace that only He can provide was mine. New day! New opportunities! Woohoo!

**Side note: I've created an extensive list of all the states and places I visited over 3+ years. You can find the list in chapter 4. I do not detail every place I visited in this book as that would be a book all of its own! **Visit my YouTube channel for an array of travel videos. You will find many of them further categorized in the playlists. {Serene and Simple Life©}

You are where God wants you to be at this very moment.
Every experience is part of His divine plan.

Coming Full Circle (Again)

You could say it has been a roller coaster of a ride since the onset of my land hunt. It's like coming full circle when I made the decision to lease land, buy a totally built-out tiny cabin on wheels, and place it in a community as I had first imagined back in Texas.

Before being shown something that made more sense in the interim, I had initially believed buying land was what I wanted and needed to do. Once again, God showed me He had something better in mind! After such an intense and time-consuming search for land, I didn't think a community like the one He brought me to existed. Early on in my journey, I compiled a written list titled "Top 10 Reasons to Buy Land."

1. No rent! Savings!
2. Pass on to children
3. Conducting car workshops
4. Serenity
5. Simplicity
6. Security
7. Sound investment
8. Something new
9. Scenery
10. Seeking God's best

{Top 10 Reasons: Zero interest in renting land}

As I look over this list, almost every one of these reasons to buy land is being met in my decision to lease land—for now. {Lease over buy land: all my needs and wants met}

Marvelous and miraculous! Perhaps number one doesn't make sense to you. "No rent!" In my mind, you don't rent land, you lease it. It's a minor play on words. Of course you may be thinking, well renting or leasing is the same thing. But to me, it's not. Renting to me is like what I did for years and years, where I rented an apartment or rented a room. I guess you could say the word has a negative connotation attached to it and I always choose positive over negative thinking! It's a simple mind-over-matter way of thinking which makes me happy.

Numbers two and seven—pass on to my children and a sound investment won't be fully achieved until the day comes when I own my land. You could say they are halfway met since I own my tiny cabin outright! The other reasons on the list are self-explanatory.

Additionally, leasing land is also nowhere near the expense of renting an apartment. I crunched the numbers of how I could justify the lease expense in my mind. I was able to cut the cost to less than half of what the actual charge would be. I considered things like water, trash, landscaping, amenities—all inclusive in leasing over owning land. Property tax was taken into consideration too. In the end, I factored the costs associated with both to warrant the money I would be spending to lease a lot. For now, the tiny cabin would be a single, sound investment.

A new chapter will begin once I move into my cabin. I look forward to being grounded for a while to refresh, regroup and refuel. This cabin would be on wheels too! God knew His child was not to be content on a permanent foundation.

Your way God, not mine.

Nomad ~ Tiny Cabin Life

Even though I've wanted a permanent place to "go home" when I desired a change of pace since the onset of this car dwelling life, the idea of being back in a semi-permanent structure for 3, 6, 12 months, or more felt unsettling to my blossoming, gypsy nomad soul. Now that I have lived in an unconventional way and loved it so much, it was truly difficult for me to imagine living within the confines of four walls with modern conveniences steps away for any length of time. However, I knew in my heart living in a tiny-country-cabin in the woods would have an inviting appeal of its own.

Early on I pictured myself on my screened porch, sitting in my rocker with heartwarming memories to fill me up and captivated by nature all around me. It would be delightful to go to bed with the white noise of a forest full of chattering crickets and wake up to the sound of birds happily chirping with each other. Daily quiet time and Bible reading on my porch nestled in the woods, overlooking the mountains, would provide a perfect ambiance to kick start each day!

Painting on canvas, framing photos taken on my journey, and selling my product at farmer's markets made the list of things to do to replace my time sightseeing across the USA. Picking up my newly acquired crochet skills as I did at Red Bridge campsite when I was adjusting to being in one place might be a worthwhile pastime to add to the "list."

Creating several digital photo albums of this unique chapter of my life and having them bound into keepsake books to add to my collection will be a worthwhile hobby. Not only will they be great resources to introduce at future meet-ups and workshops, but they will also be delightful to share with others to encourage and inspire with a complete photo documentation of my time as a nomad.

Who knows, I may even gravitate towards reading again as I did while solo camping. Incorporating daily energetic walks into my stationary routine like I once did will fill the void of challenging long hikes I went on in unknown places.

Planting flowers and even having a little garden to tend to will occupy more time. Mom had a green thumb with beautiful flower baskets she lovingly tended to. Perhaps I will see if I can emulate a little bit of the beauty she created around our home growing up.

Dad had a thriving garden he was proud of and rightfully so. Who knows, maybe I can reignite some of those long-ago memories with a vegetable garden of my own. It will certainly be worth giving it a try! Some of these activities may not come to fruition until I have land of my own.

Each day there will be new opportunities and challenges. Like anything different from the norm, it will be an adjustment at first. I imagine there will be days when it will feel especially quiet or lonely feelings may try to creep in as they did in my former life. When this happens, I will use "catch and release," —acknowledging and then releasing the feeling, for "this too shall pass." Sitting on my porch gazing at the vast mountains in the distance as a new season ushers in is something that will require no effort and will provide the necessary company I need!

Welcoming family and friends with an open invitation is something I look forward to. It is hard to have people visit when you keep moving. They will be able to locate me now!

Sometimes I think about what it would be like to be in a relationship again. Funny thing is, 20 years ago I wrote those same thoughts towards the end of my first published book: {"Rising from the Ruins; A Single Mom Takes Flight."} Now, the same notion is surfacing again. You never know what the future holds.

I am content being on my own because I know I'm not ever really alone as God is always with me. Even though companionship would be very nice, I choose to be happy with my life as it is and live in the moment.

In case you're wondering, I don't plan on giving up the nomad life. When I'm feeling restless or like the walls are closing in on me, I will head back out to explore. The thought has crossed my mind to travel for one week out of each month to GO SEE DO and be able to check off more sights on the never-ending list! This will provide me the fix I need to go and continue to explore this beautiful country God has given us for this flash of time we have here on this earth.

However, this may be another desire that will be put on the back burner until I own my property and don't have a lease payment. It will be easier at that time to afford the extra expense of traveling. I'm pretty certain the past three years have filled the GO SEE DO need for now.

At some point, I may consider putting together workshops to teach others about living in a car/SUV, in a serene and simple way. My initial idea is to host a group of 10-15 like-minded nomads where we would meet up at a park or campground. We'll camp for a few days while bonding and learning how this life could be your ticket to a new beginning of "living life large" in the great unknown. Just an idea for now, but I envision doing this in a few different locations across the country.

Oh, what fun to hang out, create, and just be! Seizing the day with little wonders of sights and sounds will fill my time, as they most certainly had during my years as a full-time nomad. As I got closer to the reality of once again living the conventional way I couldn't help but think about what lies ahead. Like always, I will take it one day at a time, living life in the moment. I feel at peace in my soul. God continues to revive my spirit and strengthen my resolve as I turn the page and He prepares me for a new chapter.

Thank you for joining me on this journey here—subscribing to my YouTube channel or my blog. In conclusion, in this portion, of sharing my personal "rut to revival" story I hope and pray that I have empowered and inspired you to live your best life in some small (or big) way. Living your best life to me is the same as "living life large" no matter what your situation or circumstances may be. Godspeed.

Life is to be enjoyed, not endured.

Chapter 8

Who I Am — What I Know

Discoveries: Learning ~ Growing

Throughout this nomadic journey of travels, work, adventures, experiences, and friends I have given some careful consideration to what I have learned about myself and how I have grown as a person.

Again, being the list maker that I am, I came up with 10 facts about my mental and emotional well-being, including how I feel now compared to days gone by living in a house. It's important to me to be self-aware and continue to strive to better myself.

In no particular order of significance, here's what I know and have learned:

1. I have learned to be more patient with myself when obstacles and unexpected circumstances occur along the journey. For example, when the weather doesn't cooperate, I have learned to go with the flow and adjust plans. Growing in patience gives me better opportunities to listen and wait on God.

2. I like living a minimalist lifestyle. It's freeing to only possess things I use or have a fondness for. Gone are the days of having too much stuff and keeping items because I believe I might need them someday.

3. I continue to be a planner and goal setter, but without the anxiety and stress that used to come with things like finishing a project related to business or simply to check it off my list.

4. I live so frugally that I no longer concern myself about making money in relation to my business.
5. Making new friends is both fun and desirable. Especially friends who understand and get you in this lifestyle.
6. I feel a new vigor and zest for life. God used me one person, one day at a time. This gives me purpose and meaning. I'm thankful for the new people He puts in my life.
7. Having a saving's account helps you sleep better at night.
8. Lonely feelings don't come to visit very often like they used to. When they do I have an antidote—GO SEE DO.
9. I look forward to a new journey of new memories which includes revisiting places I've already been and finding new sightseeing treasures.
10. I feel a renewed strength in what I'm capable of doing and called to do. I trust our creator more each day.

Nature is cheaper than therapy.

A Gypsy Soul ~ Nomad

Sometimes you must face the facts. For me, I've never been one to stay in one place for very long. History is my proof. "The best predictor of future behavior is past behavior," has been attributed to everyone from psychologists, such as Albert Ellis, Walter Michel, and B.F. Skinner, to writers such as Mark Twain. I have moved to a new residence 25 times since age 18. I did run away once when I was 12 or so with a few belongings to my BFF's house about a mile away. Not sure if that counts.

Throughout the 12 years leading up to becoming a nomad, I had moved 14 times. Over the course of 45 years, this would equate to moving once every two and a half years, give or take. I guess you could say I was preparing myself for adventures yet to come.

While raising my children as a single mom we only moved twice over 16 years. It was great to stay put during those years as I built a business and wanted my children to have the same stability I had growing up without the upheaval that moving sometimes creates.

I realize the term "gypsy" has different meanings. Some positive, others not so much. I looked up the words "gypsy soul" as I like to refer to myself. In *Wild Heart; Gypsy Soul*, it states "a person in need of change or an adventure. A gypsy seeks the next best thing in any situation. They can be very passionate and inspired by different ideas, attitudes, and experiences. Sure, gypsy souls have a wild heart."

As for being a "nomad," I checked out this definition as well. The *Urban Dictionary* defines a nomad as "N. 1. one without a home who moves around freely without ties holding them back. 2. a constant or full-time traveler."

I think both definitions fit me well. If you put them both together, I'm a gypsy soul nomad! Throughout this adventure, I have explored 40 states, traveled well over 50,000 miles—visited at least 24 national parks and monuments, plus an abundance of state parks, cities, and free attractions.

My daughter presented me with a lovely gift at Christmas time during my first year as a nomad. It is a silver bar with the words "gypsy soul" inscribed on the metal. It is entwined with a rawhide strip that wraps around my wrist. I wore it as if it were part of me for a long time. I had no idea she "got it" about her mom.

Here is some additional trivia:

- Over the course of the first 19 weeks after leaving a life of living at a permanent address, I lived in 18 different cities in Texas within a 200-mile radius while doing craft shows.

- Lived in five different cities on BLM land when I took off for the biggest adventure of my life which began in Arizona.

Now, I'll have a fixed address to call home once more, along with my SUV. I never imagined myself as one of those people who would own two homes. If my gypsy soul yearns for the open road, I'll give in.

In closing, I hope you got more out of my rut to revival story than you came here for. It is my wish that you are inspired, encouraged, and empowered to live your life to the fullest, however this looks for you. Life passes us by in an instant. If you are still able, GO SEE DO without delay. If not, hopefully you will find the smallest of things within your surroundings to provide you with a living in the moment experience.

There is beauty to behold outside your front door, whether it is on wheels or not. Inhale the fresh air and slowly exhale. That is something your body requires. Open your eyes and ears to sights and sounds that you may have previously taken for granted. We have been promised nothing more than this very moment. Gratitude and joy are your companions. We all have had some rough patches in our lives, but this doesn't mean your story can't end happily ever after. Never look back after turning the page.

I wish you God's greatest and abundant blessings because our Father God loves to bless His children. Perhaps you, too, will opt for a more liberated way of life, complete with a new or refreshed sense of serenity and simplicity.

TRUST in the Lord with all your heart and
He will direct your path ~ Proverbs 3:5-6

My Top 10 Whys ~ Nomad Lifestyle

Before embarking on a full-time journey into the great unknown, I jotted down my top 10 reasons for leaving a stationary life confined by four walls. Living as a nomad was an unparalleled option for me. It was important to me to live my life to the fullest and give it all my attention. Years later, I've lived out and continue to fulfill my top 10 reasons. But now, I changed the initial wording of this list from "I'm going to" to "I am."

1. I am living by myself, not in someone else's home with their rules dictating to me how I should do things. As the saying goes, I am "free as a bird."
2. I am most fulfilled outdoors in God's green earth. When I was living in a house I designed products on my porch and participated in outdoor art/craft shows just to "live" outside. A common statement of vehicle dwellers is "we don't live in our vehicle, we live outside our vehicle."
3. I am "enlarging my territory" all for God's glory. To me the way I can accomplish this is to take the business and ministry He has given me and share it with as many people as I can. Whether it be the "how to" of living in a car or by sharing daily inspiration, I can reach many more people as I travel the country.
4. I am accomplishing a passion of mine to travel and see the country in a way I can afford. No motels, hotels, or paid recreation sites. I am living rent-free for the first time in over 45 years.
5. I am living the American dream. I own my two homes with no mortgages attached. I am free from the banks.
6. I am daily practicing a "less is more" philosophy/ mentality.
7. I am expanding my connection with people and making many new friends. The experience is providing me with a tribe of like-minded people. To me, this realizes a universal need we all have,

to be accepted and loved. It is a priceless journey to meet people from all walks of life with a story all their own.

8. I am walking the talk. By this I mean, while having a career in the direct sales industry, I coached my team of consultants to step out of their comfort zone. This lifestyle is no exception, and I am embracing living out of my comfort zone once again.

9. I am strengthening and building faith muscle as I choose faith over fear in every circumstance and challenge that comes my way, including, being up close and personal with an elk. Yikes! {Up close and personal encounter}

10. Lastly, I am living life in the moment and being in the present without distraction, filling up my heart with precious memories, longer conversations with people without feeling rushed to be somewhere, just chilling while crocheting beanies for the homeless, reading or writing.

How Long Will I Do This?

It's always too soon to quit! Years ago, at a business convention I attended, a keynote speaker shared these very words. This phrase stuck with me on my journey.

As I backed out of the driveway of my one room abode for the final time I committed to at least one year of traveling and living out of my car barring any unforeseen circumstances. Why? I'm convinced you need to give yourself a chance to learn the "how to" when you decide to do something you've never done before—such as living in a car. It's almost impossible to determine if your decision is going to pan out in a brief time. Besides, anything that seems to be hard today may be quite easy the more you do, learn, and put effort into it. And who knows you may grow to love your new life decisions and never look back!

Not only am I glad I stuck with my conviction but I'm elated that I gave myself the time needed to see the beauty of this spectacular countryside, the USA. I believe it vital to give the Lord a chance to use you as He may, putting people in your path as you go and providing you with new opportunities. We can't rush God or put Him on a timeline but we can recognize it's always too soon to quit!

As for me, the commitment I made to myself was a year for starters to adjust to something brand new and unconventional! Who knew that it would be over three years living in a car, for my first journey out into the great unknown!

Nature Soothes the Soul

Awareness ~ Life in the Moment

Over the years, it's been the little things in life, tangible or not which have brought me the most joy. I paid extra attention while living the nomad life to take my time to live simply in the present, letting go of hastily moving from one place to the next. Being cognizant of how I have navigated in the past, I knew I had a better chance of not missing anything along the way.

I've always been aware of the importance of living in the moment, but it hasn't always come naturally or without effort. Deadlines, continuous errands, and never-ending to-do lists were once part of my daily routine. I spent a significant portion of my life living in a hurried state, dashing from one task to the next to check off the list before falling into bed exhausted each night. The additional pressure of building a successful direct sales business provided its own challenge to slow down and savor the moment.

That pesky list of things to do seemed to talk to me. I put forth a good effort to turn down the volume in my head and not be distracted when I was engaging with others. Knowing the days are long, but the years are short when it comes to raising children, it was equally important for me to not let special moments of us together slip by without being fully present. Thankfully, at times I was able to slow up what felt like a fast-moving train to make some wonderful memories.

My heart was full as I recalled some things our little family of three enjoyed: going to the nearby local pool, having a simple picnic in a peaceful park, dropping in at our huge local library to pick out some VCR tapes for a Friday movie night, riding bikes down a long narrow dirt trail to a lively park, having fun-filled game nights—all the while being silly and devouring pizza. Here you have a few examples of the simple, uncomplicated times in my life. These activities provided opportunities to be present and carefree. I imagine you can make your own list of simple yet significant times of "living in the moment." Try it; it's validating!

In my former traditional lifestyle, I especially embraced the moment with elation when receiving things like drawings, photos, cards, and notes from my kids, family, business associates, and friends. As you know I had a ton of these pieces to go through when I hit up my stash of mementos! Everything swirling around me seemed to pause for a minute when I opened cheerful correspondence!

Like I mentioned, there were plenty of times throughout my life when it felt more like I was living a life of survival rather than genuinely presiding in the moment. Thankfully God gives us second and third chances to get it right!

You may be wondering what all of this reminiscing about days gone by has to do with the nomad life. Looking back and remembering makes me realize two things—Firstly, I know I'm capable of living in the moment and secondly, I can take what I learned from the past and become even more keenly aware of what I am doing and how I am choosing to navigate my days now.

Like in sticks and bricks, on the road I received thank you notes and drawings from my grand sweet peas. My generous sister sent me thoughtful care packages. I was overjoyed when I received mail either from my mail forwarding address or general delivery through the local post office when passing through. Stationary or not, talking on the phone, in-person conversations, text and video chats with those near and dear to me have their own special way of being able to stay in the moment.

Out amongst nature for years provided its own kind of specialties to be fully engaged. Simple moments like viewing the first signs of spring in Utah, compacted snow left over from a harsh winter in Mt Rainier, and even the sound of rain beating down on my home sweet home—filled my senses and slowed up my over-active brain!

It seems as I get older most of my time is being spent mindfully living in the present. Oh, the entrepreneur in me is very much alive, but it is at a slower pace. I no longer have any lofty goals, such as building a substantial business, or mortgage payments that tacked on additional stress.

My short- and long-term goals are now intertwined with a great deal of flexibility. The fact that I have chosen to live a prudent lifestyle allows me to avoid the pressure of the past to succeed.

At my leisure, I go for a brisk walk or an easy to moderate hike. It's a great way to exercise your body and clear your mind of worries. There are times when I sit down at a picnic table and cook up a simple meal on my portable gas stove. I watch the world go by—people watching, squirrels, birds, ducks, seagulls; you name it! I take tons of photos and vlog all my adventures.

If I'm starved I find a fast-food joint to grab and go while driving. Admittedly, I don't slow up to savor a messy taco or hot french fries! They're gone in no time, but the feeling of gratitude that I can afford to do this occasional splurge is there. When taking a long shower, the warm water revives my physical body and melts away any stress I'm carrying.

As I continue my journey, the opportunities to be present and seize the day are unlimited. Knowing that I recognize what makes life even more precious makes this nomad's life so much more rewarding.

On your journey, I hope you'll find that it's uplifting to keep discovering the little things in life that will bring you the most joy and fulfillment too. The best part is the more you discover the more you want to keep doing and going!

Live for today. Tomorrow is not promised.

Self-Induced Stress

At times having a YouTube channel has been a time-consuming and occasionally stressful endeavor, even though I genuinely enjoy sharing and interacting with my viewers. Many of you have become my friends, and I'm so appreciative you want to hear from the "babbling brook."

Planning shows in advance, shooting videos almost daily, and scheduling anywhere between three to five videos per week consistently to maintain my channel's growth, I put unnecessary pressure on myself. Running out of storage space on my device to create new content was at times a challenge. Deleting videos to open up storage space and chasing a strong signal to upload new shows was a constant activity that contributed to stressful moments. It was only after I had finished editing, uploading, and scheduling the publication of the videos, that I would breathe again and stop to smell the coffee. Or is that roses?

My Say It Display It® business had its own demands when it came to filling orders. I put undue stress on myself to get orders out as soon as possible as a good business practice. Since I only carry a small amount of inventory with me when I travel, I frequently had backorders to fill at the storage unit where I housed my product in Texas.

But for the most part, my days are filled with both fun work and frequent play. Usually, my work is my play. I feel upbeat when I'm active and productive. I've combated some of these work-related stressors by tuning in to the sounds of the birds while drinking my morning coffee and planning my day—plan your work, work your plan!

There are numerous ways to chill without stress interfering. To me, nature and the outdoors provide the balance I strive for. Paying attention to what my stressors are and what I can do to alleviate them helps me to maintain good health—emotional, mental, physical and spiritual!

And into the forest,
I go to lose my mind and find my soul.

Gratitude Changes Everything

I once read it doesn't matter what you have in life (i.e., a big house, fancy car, nice clothes), but rather who you have beside you in your life. I think you'd agree that relationships with others are much more important than things. I also believe how you view your life is influenced by how you use and enjoy the things you have, not how many material possessions you have.

I embrace the less is more concept in this lifestyle. First, I have no room for extra stuff. Second, having lots of stuff weighs me down mentally and sometimes even emotionally, taking up rent in my head.

Every day, gratitude influences everything I do, from the blessing of a new day to enjoying a comfortable, secure landing place for the evening in my car. Millions of people around the world lack the blessings most of us have, such as a roof over our heads or a comfortable place to rest our heads at night. Being grateful is sweet nectar for your soul and makes everything valuable, even when things are hard or seem unfair.

Gratitude turns what we have into enough.

Chapter 9

How and What of Nomad Life

Clothing

The first thing I recommend when trying to figure out what to take, what to leave behind is to dig into your closet and pull out your absolute necessities—things like your most comfortable, can't live without, and easy to launder clothes. Consider clothing for varying temperatures. If you are like me, you'll have to revisit your selections and further eliminate them as you work out how much clothing suffices to meet your needs!

**I housed all my clothing in four storage systems:

1. (7) "Amazon basic" mesh bags
2. Large fabric tote bag—my stylish Vera Bradley brand!
3. Collapsible fabric box (same type I used for snacks)
4. Extra large IKEA bag

You may find all of these items in my Amazon store except for the tote bag.

One additional thing to consider—the more clothes you take with you the more laundry you have to do, though at the same time, the fewer clothes you have the more often you'll need to do laundry. It's a decision only you can make. As you can see from the list below I carried quite a few tops with me for two reasons—less often at the laundromat which equated to saving money and simply because I like lots of color choices! I stretched the time between laundromat visits, wearing most pieces multiple times. Deodorant helps! There were times when I hand-washed my undergarments to save a little chunk of change as they were always the first I'd run out of. As my dad used to say "it all adds up!" I made going to the laundromat a fun, eventful time. Doing laundry always seemed to take up a good portion of the day, so why not have fun! I struck up some interesting conversations while there and even met a couple of owners along the way! {Laundry day ~ so much more}

My list of essentials	**Jot Down Your Thoughts on Clothes to Go**
Cold Weather	
flannel bottoms	
fleece jacket	
long john sets (2)	
long sleeve tops (4)	
loose joggers	
pair of jeans	
sweatshirt	
sweatshirt jacket	
wool socks (2)	
Warm Weather	
jean capris (2)	
jean shorts	
knit shorts (5)	
knit skirt	
short sleeve tops (8)	
skort	
stretchy workout capris (2)	

My list of essentials	**Jot Down Your Thoughts on Clothes to Go**
tank tops (10)	
Miscellaneous	
capri pjs (2)	
sleep shirts (2)	
socks (5)	
undergarments (15)	

Power

How does one manage as a full-time car dweller without wires scattered everywhere! I admit the thought of full-time car dwelling without having wall outlets was daunting when I decided to hit the road full-time in my Acura. How would I power my laptop, iPad, kindle, iPhone, fan, light, and more?

I spent a lot of time researching, watching videos, and asking questions in various social media groups. The answers came one by one as I considered space limitations in my car, ease of use of different power items, and how much it would all cost. {Power it all up!}

Four main items enabled me to maintain sufficient power for my devices mentioned above.

Jackery lithium battery bank: referred to as an all-in-one plug and play, two USB ports, an AC plug, 12 Volt, DC

Jackery 50-watt solar panel: pairs with the Jackery battery bank. Over the course of eight hours in full sunlight, the Jackery battery bank can be fully charged. It also has a USB port built-in. There are times I utilize a sunny day to not only charge my battery bank backup but to also charge my iPhone or portable battery bank as well. The sun does its thing and I have fully-charged devices. I could never have imagined I'd be living in a time of solar energy let alone relying on and using it to power up a battery bank. I must mention it was a very thoughtful and generous gift from my son. Gotta love sunshine and thoughtful kids!

Anker brand battery bank: consists of two USB ports to charge my phone six to eight times. It's very cool as there are four light-up dots to see the level of charge capacity.

Best Tek brand 300-watt inverter: when on a long road trip, I plug the inverter into my cigarette lighter, then plug whatever needs charging into the inverter. The inverter has one AC outlet for the laptop or Jackery plus two USB ports.

That's it! Simple and easy to understand, space savers and ready in an instant to use anytime. It wasn't always this simple. I had days when I would get confused about what's what. Overall, like anything, I have found the more you use something the more accustomed and easier it gets.

Disclaimer: I'm an Amazon influencer and receive a small percentage of what you purchase by shopping from my {Amazon Store} (links also in the description of videos on my YouTube channel). You can locate all the power items and over 150 other products I have incorporated into both of my homes on wheels! You don't even have to purchase the exact item(s) listed within my store. The only Amazon requirement is that whatever you put in your shopping cart from the link needs to be ordered within 24 hours. There is no extra charge to you, and I receive a small commission. It's like a thank you from them and I in return **thank you!**

I encourage you to start with the bare minimums like I did if trying to figure out all this power stuff intimidates you. You can always add more power or solar to your rig as you go. We are in a fascinating era of many different options to power up your devices. Go forth and power on!

Hygiene

One of my major concerns in choosing to live full-time on the road was how would I stay clean and where would I fill the need for a hot shower? I finally figured it out. It is possible to stay and feel fresh and clean even when there is no access to a shower.

3 Ways to Stay Clean
GOOD ~ BETTER ~ BEST

(1) GOOD – baby wipes, quick and easy, daily wash
(2) BETTER – large spray bottle and basin, shower bag with a hose
(3) BEST – showers are my go-tos while traveling and you can find them at:

- ❖ Hostel
- ❖ Recreation Center
- ❖ State Park
- ❖ Truck stops
- ❖ YMCA

Tip: ask your internet search engine "showers near me"

I've always believed anything is possible if you want it badly enough. I was bound and determined to leave behind a life of mortgages and rent that, as my father used to say—kept him in the poor house. I've discovered a way to be clean, feel clean, and stay clean without taking regular showers. I hardly ever miss them. But when I have access to one, it provides me some instant relaxation for the day. When you are lacking something, you tend to appreciate it, even more, when it comes your way.

Check out the {hygiene} and {makeup} videos from the series, "Short and Sweet Saturday – food-power-clothing-hygiene-makeup."

Budget

Many people are curious about what you need financially to live life as a nomad. Of course, as different as it is for everyone in a stationary home, the same will be true in this nomadic lifestyle. I can honestly say I am living a large life with a small budget.

As you are probably aware by now, I am thrifty and watch most of my pennies. It wasn't always like this for me. I lived outside my means with that dangerous plastic called credit cards. Earlier I shared that as an entrepreneur I also dumped money into businesses thinking they would grow faster. But in reality, I was on a vicious treadmill leading to more debt and more financial stress.

When I was able to eliminate my debt, I could finally breathe, start over, and learn from my mistakes. I can live within my means now without working my life away just to pay the bills and make ends meet. Hallelujah!

Without rent or mortgage payments and no credit card bills, I sleep better at night.

Average Monthly Budget Overview*	
Car insurance:	$85
Car maintenance: (oil changes)	$21
Dentist: (2x a year)	$17
Eating out: (fast food)	$50
Food:	$175
Gasoline:	$200
Gifts:	$60
Haircut: (4x a year)	$10
Miscellaneous: (hygiene, paper goods)	$20
National park pass:	$7
Phone:	$76
Storage unit:	$50
Treats:	$20
Website:	$35
Total monthly expenses:	$826

*These amounts were based on the years I was traveling. I did not include the $75 state park pass as that was not purchased till years later.

{Budget for a nomad}

No rent or mortgage, no entertainment expenses—only partaking in "FREE," except for the yearly national park pass, no restaurant meals except occasional fast food, no utilities, and no clothing budget.

Picking up side jobs while traveling (see work chapter 6), alongside my business has provided me with a necessary cushion of three to six months of savings to cover monthly expenses in case of an emergency and unexpected occurrences like car repairs. My expenses are minimal. I didn't have much wiggle room, though I was living life large. A frugal lifestyle is possible while experiencing the joy of traveling.

There were times I stopped at fast food places while traveling many hundreds of miles to reach my next destination though this splurge was far and few between. So many choices—Burger King, McDonald's, Wendy's, Taco Bell, Chick-fil-A. Sometimes I found it hard to decide where to eat when I was famished. It was fun to switch up and I loved the variety.

I hope that you can gather from the breakdown of my budget and story that you can thrive and not just survive while living full time on the road or simply anywhere. You may need to give up little luxuries that add up and replace them with free adventures instead! Make your days count with new experiences, not stuff.

Cast all your anxiety on Him because
He cares for you ~ 1 Peter 5:7

Sleep: In a Car ~ In an SUV

When an individual sees the set up of my home, most often the first question they ask is, "where do you sleep?" They don't see a cot, mattress, or even the space needed to stretch out.

"I sleep in the driver's seat in a reclining position" is my one-liner answer. They usually look at me like I've pretty much lost my mind until

I assure them it is by choice, and I sleep very well. That also means no aches or pains to work through in the morning or ever. What an anomaly!

Believe it or not, I have been quite comfortable both sleeping first in the comfort of luxurious, leather seats in the Acura which had lumbar support built in, and now in the Toyota Highlander. It's not quite as plush so I purchased a substitute cushion for my back and a gel-type cushion for the seat. They work!

At first, I only had a travel pillow, which was gifted to me by a friend, and a small accent pillow to cushion the side door that I rested up against.

Later, I added two squishy balls made of soft fabric and filled with pillow stuffing. I picked them up on two different occasions with my discount from Walmart. They are a nice decor touch too. One is a small multi-white/gray and the other is a large, light-gray color. You may have seen them at Christmas time in large bins parked in the middle of the store in the main aisle. You know, one of those strategically placed items for impulse buys. They got me and have been a lifesaver. The small one rests alongside the driver-side door, and the large one is positioned over the console at night to stretch out and rest my legs on.

In addition to the pillows and squishy balls, I purchased a rectangular wedge form to cover the seat belt mechanism. This was a necessity as digging one's back into a hard plastic seat belt contraption is very uncomfortable! I have perfected my nightly setup to make it as cozy and snug as possible. Pillows and cushions of various sizes and shapes provide just that!

{Sleeping demonstration in Car} and {Sleeping in the front seat of an SUV}

For the most part, I'm a side sleeper. With this strategic pillow set up, I stretch my legs out sideways across the console or I curl up in a fetal position. I've adapted and it's quite agreeable to me. There have been a few folks who have commented about dealing with poor circulation or swollen ankles. I haven't experienced either issue. Maybe it's about how you position yourself.

My co-pilot Andy the stuffed bear is a smiley cuddle. On those cold nights, he provides warmth too. Viewing the sun go down from my picture window in the front driver's seat provides a serene setting for sweet dreams. Does it get any better than that?

Now you may ask, why not a bed? Many, if not all nomads, build or set up some kind of bed structure in their minivan, car, or SUV which is simple enough when you take out the seats. I guess you could say I'm just different! Do you have someone in your life who likes to sleep in a recliner or must sleep that way due to a particular health issue?

My mom chose a recliner later in life because of back and hip issues. Like mother, like daughter as the saying goes only for different reasons. As mentioned early on, when I slept in a bed, I would get an unusual pain underneath my rib cage when I would adjust my body from side to side. It only lasted a few seconds, though by morning it necessitated applying heat to relax my muscles. Doctors were clueless but I figured out how to get a restful night's sleep!

Moral of this dilemma—I'm much more comfortable in a reclining position and much happier in the morning too. Who would've known living in my car would be a blessing in disguise to get out of a bed and into a chair! Sunsets and a night of sound sleep, just doesn't get any better than that. {Bed or chair? And the winner is?!}

Sometimes overcoming a challenge is as simple as changing the way you think about it.

Top 10 Basic Essentials

Here are the top 10 essentials on my list for life on the road as a nomad which all fit, plus, I've included a few luxuries.

1. Steering wheel table
2. Collapsible camp-style metal table
3. Collapsible potty
4. Gas One butane OR propane stove
5. *Pop-up dressing/potty room/shower
6. Two medium size and four combo packs- large, mead, small, narrow soft-sided zipper bags
7. 90% Wool blanket
8. Clip-on night light for reading and/or ambiance
9. Rechargeable LED book light, neck hug light
10. 12-volt hot water pot

*The pop-up dressing room wore out with the strong winds in Arizona and has been replaced by a clam shelter that I love!

Tip: watch this video to see a live visual overview. {Top ten essentials}

Top 5 Safety Essentials

1. Tire gauge
2. Sabre 3-in-1 pepper spray -police strength, compact size with clip, stand-alone unit

3. Seven in one tool flashlight, red blinker light, magnetic to display on the outside of your rig, seat belt cutter, window breaker, crank charger with USB port when no power. Carry this tool so you never will need it!
4. Swiss army knife
5. Red mini flashlight for night

{Top five safety essentials}

Fun video of my kid's support of mom's unconventional lifestyle: {Kid's support with thoughtful gifts}

Luxuries or Necessities?

1. Power Supply Jackery 240 lithium battery power
2. Jackery 50-watt solar panel
3. 300-watt inverter with two USB and 110 adapter
4. External battery bank for 6-8 phones or other devices charger

{Top luxuries/necessities car dweller}

I hope this overview of my essentials, luxuries, and safety tools will be of help and empower you on your journey, whether you are already out there, thinking about it, or even sharing with a friend who may benefit from having this information.

Great things never came from comfort zones.

Food Haul: Staples ~ Quick and Simple

On average, I generally carried at least two weeks of food with me. I had two different storage systems for canned goods:

1. **Car:** (2) plastic bins with lids
2. **SUV:** Two drawers locking stackable unit

Snacks were housed in a collapsible fabric box on the front seat. It was a handy place for those snack attacks while driving. Grab and eat! Sometimes I had an overflow of munchies. I'd store bigger, loose bags of chips in the back or on the floor. Outta sight, outta mind for a while. Usually, I'd only open one, maybe two bags of anything at a time. I liked buying in excess as I found I would save money with fewer trips to the store, therefore eliminating impulse buys. Not to mention the variety of food I constantly had at my fingertips!

Simple eating for a meal: Fast ~ Faster ~ Fastest

Fast: Take a can of meat, a vegetable and either a rice or noodle pack, (see list below) stir together, and heat up in a stainless steel two-quart pot or a Teflon fry pan. Within minutes you'll have a tasty meal for a lunch/dinner combo and sometimes even leftovers for the next day. I have fun making casseroles just like I did when raising my children. Only this type of meal is a one-minute mix together and three-minute heat up instead of 45 minutes baking in the oven.

Another quick and fun meal to make is tasty nachos using bean with bacon soup. Dilute soup with a half can of water, heat, and spoon onto a plate of nachos, or eat as a dip.

Faster: Cans!

My Pantry	Jot Your Thoughts on a Pantry to Go
All-In-One Meals	
Beef stew	
Chicken and dumplings	
Chili with or without beans	
Enchiladas	
La Choy stir fry vegetables	
Soup	
Bean with bacon	
Chicken and rice	
Chicken and vegetables	
Clam chowder	
Cream of potato	
Home-style chicken noodle	
Sirloin burger and vegetables	
Split pea and ham	
Vegetable	
Vegetable beef	

Fastest: No refrigeration or stove required!

- chicken salad, salmon, tuna foil packs
- chicken, devil ham, tuna, in a can for sandwiches
- cheez whiz and crackers, peanut butter with a piece of fruit

Additional food I had on hand—variety is the spice of life!

My Pantry	Jot Your Thoughts on a Pantry to Go
Meat	
Chicken	
Crab	
Ham	
Roast beef	
Salmon	
Shrimp	
Tuna	

Vegetables	
Beets	
Carrots	
Corn	
Diced potatoes	
French green beans	
Green beans	
Lima beans	
Mushrooms	
Peas	
Peas and carrots	
Rice Packs	
Basmati	
Brown	
Chicken fried	
Jasmine	
Vegetable fried	
Wild grain	
Noodle Packs	
Alfredo	
Broccoli	
Butter	
Chicken flavor	
Fruit Cups	
Applesauce	
Mandarin oranges	
Mango	
Peaches	
Pears	
Snacks	
Cereal (Cheerios, Oatmeal Squares,	
Rice Chex)	
Chips (potato, tortilla)	
Crackers (Cheez It, Ritz, Saltines,	
Triscuit, Wheat thins)	
Dried fruit (apricots, mangos, prunes raisins,)	
Fresh Fruit (apples, avocados, bananas, grapes, nectarines, peaches, pears, plums)	

Granola bars	
Nuts (cashews, peanuts, pecans, walnuts)	
Power bars	
Pretzels	
Rice cakes	
Breakfast	
Eggs	
Granola	
Hash (can)	
Instant Oatmeal	
Muffins	
Sweet rolls	
Tortillas	

Fun videos of my food hauls:

- A prepper? Walmart haul
- Shopping again: a big one!
- Trader Joe before a long road trip

More fun videos of some meals:

- Casserole crazy
- Casserole sample
- Food I carried in Serenity Sedan
- What do I eat?

Do what brings you the most joy

Chapter 10

Nomad Life Bonus

Sticks and Bricks to Nomad Lifestyle**

TOP 12 Shows to Get You Going (duplicates of videos interspersed throughout book)

1. Top Ten essentials car dwelling
2. Part ll Necessities/luxuries
3. Part lll Safety Essentials
4. Budget time
5. Bravery Faith Trust
6. FOOD: fast faster fastest
7. POWER to power everything
8. Clothes, clothes, and more clothes
9. Hygiene: No fuss no muss good better best
10. Minimalism: talk at 2020 RTR
11. Window coverings
12. Bedtime homes: suburbs, cities, and more

Bonus

- Continuation of where do I sleep, Knocks

Up Close and Personal

Feel sorry for this full-time SUV dwelling granny?
The Big reveal
Top 10 lifestyle changes

What is Serene and simple life's purpose
Why would you choose to live in a car
Your questions my answers

Top 3 Most Viewed Video/Shows

- My personal story
- #1 Burning Question
- My children: my life their life

**All videos referenced in this chapter may be found at the Serene and Simple Life YouTube channel in the playlists under the specific headings listed here.

Let go of all that keeps you from living now.

Joy In the Journey: It's All Here!

I wrote this poem a few weeks before I embarked on this serene and simple life nomad journey. I sent it to family and friends to explain and highlight what I was about to do.

She is Me

There is this different woman who lives in a car.
She travels around with Andy the bear and has plans to go far.
To beaches, forests, and views to admire.
Of freedom and peace, she never shall tire.
Some think she has lost her mind.
Along this journey who knows what she'll find!
She will meet new folk, craft, work, and dare to explore.
And then the next day she'll want to do more.
God is at the wheel, navigating the road.
Faith as her wings to lighten the load.
She desires to make a difference along the way.

He used her to serve others throughout her days.
Her motto is all we are given is today.
To embrace and enjoy as we may.
Gratitude is her mindset.
Prayers are appreciated, she will take all she can get.
She takes care of herself and feels better than ever.
When will she stop traveling?
God willing, the answer is never.

New Beginnings: Ready or Not?

	Take the Quiz (True or False)	True	False
1	I want to experience all that nature has to offer.		
2	I want to "GO SEE DO" and visit new places.		
3	I'm fine being by myself.		
4	I want to live my own life and not lean on others to fulfill my happiness.		
5	Approval from others when I embark on something new is not something I need to accomplish my goals and dreams, though it would be nice if I had it.		
6	I prefer memories over stuff any day.		
7	I like to think outside the box and do things differently.		
8	Excreting bodily waste like humans did for thousands of years or finding a different way other than a flush toilet is perfectly fine by me.		
9	I like new and different over familiar and same old same old routine.		
10	Getting lost is not terrifying to me.		
11	Breaking down in a vehicle does not make me feel helpless or scared.		
12	I can eat pretty much anything to sustain me. Eating fresh and homemade is not always necessary.		
13	I have at least the recommended $3,000 as a financial buffer to pay for the unexpected. Rule of thumb: the bigger the rig the bigger the buffer.		
14	I enjoy my own company and I'm okay being alone in my thoughts.		
15	I can roll with the unexpected and use critical thinking skills as well as common sense to alleviate challenges or deal with them.		
16	My health is fine, and I know how to maneuver and manage my challenges and issues. My health doesn't stop me from living life.		
17	I don't mind change.		
18	I understand life is fleeting and want to live a life of no regrets.		
19	Saving money makes me glad and gives me a sense of security.		
20	I am not content and know there has got to be more to life than what I'm currently doing.		
	Total your true and false answers.		

How did you do?

- If you answered **FALSE** to five or more questions, you may need to stay put in your stationary home, at least for now until you work through your challenges and any issues.
- If you answered **FALSE** to 10 or more of the questions, you are not cut from the same mold as a nomad, and staying in your stationary home is most likely working for you.
- If you answered **TRUE** to at least 16 of the questions, you should investigate being a nomad and start the process of getting serious about this alternative lifestyle.
- If you answered **TRUE** to all 20 of the questions, my question to you is: what are you waiting for? It's time for you to go live life large now!

Epilogue

When I completed this book for publication, I was stationary in a tiny cabin home nestled in the woods, overlooking the mountains. This has been a time to regroup, refuel and renew my gypsy spirit. My life is indeed rich and full. I have been living serenely in my new second tiny dwelling on wheels that I named "Rocky Pine Retreat," and it's a super addition to my SUV retreat! {It's here! My tiny cabin!}

I anticipate and look forward to the next chapter of growth in my life which will be owning a piece of land to place a new tiny cabin home on as a landing zone between travels. God willing, I will continue to GO SEE DO in my SUV home to places yet unknown, experiencing yet more of God's masterpiece. Who knows, I may travel abroad again as I did in my younger years.

While living in my car I was approached by a filmmaker from Belgium about being part of a documentary on older women living a nomad life. I happily accepted. He came to my tiny cabin home and did more filming of me and my life, for his project {Filmmaker, Sebastien interviews me ~ then and now}. It is currently in the editing stages. My understanding is at some point it will be introduced at film festivals. Once I am given a link to the film I will share it—most likely on my YouTube channel. Only God knows the timeline of everything!

In the meantime, whether I am traveling or not, I am happy and content as God blesses me with yet another day here on earth.

Blessings in your day and JOY in the journey.

About the Author

Linda Mastromonaco has always had wanderlust in her being. In her book, she will take you down a long bumpy road from living a so-called "normal" life to breaking the mold and pursuing a fascinating journey covering tens of thousands of miles to fulfill tucked-away dreams and desires of years gone by.

Linda has successfully proven that you can live a life of abundance living out of a car with little money or any modern conveniences. If you want to learn in detail about living a nomad life, experience "living life large" in an unconventional way and go after your heart's desires then this book is for you. Or if you feel like your life as you know it has lost its meaning and purpose then this will be the encouragement you need to get moving.

With many years of experience as a motivational speaker and inspiring a team of thousands of consultants, she is unstoppable to guide you in specific and profound ways. Her positivity is contagious as her glass is never just half full but always overflowing with gratitude and joy.

In her first book—Rising from the Ruins; A Single Mom Takes Flight her intertwining message was "If I can do it, then by the grace of God so can you." Over twenty years later her message remains steadfast. She wishes to motivate you to explore what moves you and provides deep satisfaction for you. Her message today is—Step out in Faith, conquer fear holding you hostage to your hopes and dreams. Live a life experiencing God's best for you in every step you take on your journey!

BLESSED

Made in the USA
Monee, IL
19 May 2025